LINCOLN AT GETTYSBURG

By WILLIAM E. BARTON

THE LIFE OF ABRAHAM LINCOLN
THE WOMEN LINCOLN LOVED
ABRAHAM LINCOLN AND WALT WHITMAN
THE GREAT GOOD MAN
A BEAUTIFUL BLUNDER
THE LINEAGE OF LINCOLN
THE FATHER OF HIS COUNTRY
MY FAITH IN IMMORTALITY

LINCOLN
AT GETTYSBURG

*What He Intended to Say; What
He Said; What He Was Reported
to Have Said; What He Wished
He Had Said*

By

WILLIAM E. BARTON
Author of The Life of Abraham Lincoln

Illustrated

THE BOBBS-MERRILL COMPANY
PUBLISHERS   INDIANAPOLIS

Printed in the United States of America

PRESS OF
BRAUNWORTH & CO., INC.
BOOK MANUFACTURERS
BROOKLYN, N. Y.

To

MY DEAR FRIENDS

ROY E. AND ELEANOR TOMLINSON

Photograph of Lincoln made by Alexander Gardner at Gettysburg,
November 11, 1863

FOREWORD

BOOKS about Lincoln at Gettysburg are abundant and of value. Most of them relate at first hand the recollections of their authors who were present at Gettysburg and heard Lincoln there. My debt to these books is apparent in the pages that follow and is here further acknowledged. Probably there will never be any more books of that character. It is well that we have as many as we now possess. But no such book, however honest, tells or can tell the whole story, and that is what the present work undertakes to do. This undertaking involves the assembling of material and sitting in critical judgment upon it, a process far more difficult than most readers will be able to realize.

The Gettysburg Address was one of the most conspicuous events in Lincoln's entire career. It was heard by many thousands of people. It was reported in all the prominent newspapers of the country. Of very few of Lincoln's addresses have we a single copy in his own handwriting, and if there be two copies of any other, I do not remember to have seen them. There is no known manuscript copy of the First Inaugural, and only one of the Second Inaugural. But of the Gettysburg Address we have no less than five copies, still extant, in Lincoln's own hand, and another copy printed in the official report from manuscript furnished by him. It would seem that it should be very easy to relate just what he said and how he said it, and all else that should be of record about it. And yet there prevails a very considerable uncertainty about nearly every detail of that address. The place and method of its preparation, the manner of its delivery, the effect upon those who heard it, and the very content of the speech itself, have given rise to innumerable variations of tradition, and sharply contradictory reports on the part of those who heard. Books and magazine articles almost innumerable have professed to tell the true story of this notable oration, and they can not all be true.

As to Lincoln's preparation, it would be possible to prove that he did not make any, but trusted wholly to the inspiration of the moment; that he made hasty preparation on the morning of the delivery of the address; that he wrote his sketch on the train on the way between Washington and Gettysburg; that he wrote it on the night before its delivery; and that he wrote it in full before leaving Washington.

As to his manuscript, we could prove that he had no manuscript with him on the platform; that he had a manuscript, but that it was either a card or a piece of paper not larger than a card; that he had some notes on paper of rough appearance, presumed to have been those that he had written on the train; that he delivered his address from notes on a yellow envelope, being the same on which Governor Curtin had seen him write the night before; that he had one sheet of paper, described as note-paper and as letter-paper by different observers; that his paper was the identical paper of letter size which Judge Wills had seen in his hand the night before; that he had several sheets of paper, of typewriter size; that he took his manuscript out of his side pocket before he rose and, finding it crumpled, smoothed it out on his knee; that he rose with his manuscript in his hand; that he took his manuscript out of his breast pocket after he rose; that he began to speak with no manuscript in his hand and produced it after he had uttered one or two sentences and held it until he had finished.

As to his gestures or the lack of them, it could be proved that he held his manuscript firmly with both hands and made no gestures or other perceptible movement while speaking; that, holding his manuscript in one or the other hand, he used the free hand in gesture; that he gestured, but with movements of his body and not of his hands; and that he began with his right hand extended, gesticulated more or less freely as he proceeded, and closed with both hands uplifted as if he were in the act of pronouncing a benediction.

As to the delivery of the address, one could easily prove from persons who heard it that he delivered it without any use of manuscript; that he held a manuscript in his left hand and did not refer to it; that he held a manuscript in both hands and followed it somewhat carefully; and finally that he was closely confined to his manuscript and read every word of it.

As to the effect of its delivery, there is equally impressive proof that the address was several times interrupted by applause and that there was prolonged applause at the close; that there was applause at the close only and that it was perfunctory; that there was no applause because people who heard the address were disappointed in it; and that there was no applause because the occasion was so solemn and the address was so impressive that applause would have seemed profane.

The Gettysburg Address is so important in American history and literature, we can not afford not to know all that is to be known about it. We fortunately have abundant testimony from men who were present; and that is a part of our problem.

In considering these records of eye-witnesses, it is to be remembered that most of the men whose testimony we shall now present were men of unusual ability, many of them accustomed to delivering speeches, and to examining witnesses under oath. They were men who were then or who thereafter became prominent. No one of them had any occasion to deceive, or any motive that might seriously have warped his judgment.

Every one of them knew that the event was an occasion of importance, and no one could have regarded it with indifference. All were attentive, and each one told what he thought he remembered and what he honestly believed.

These testimonies as here given are important as showing out of what materials history may be made. And since the body of evidence here is so large, it affords profitable reflection to the effect that most history must be written on the evidence of original sources much less abundant and in the main less reliable. It would be possible to multiply this body of testimony, but to do so would only give us added contradiction of details, and this feature is adequately illustrated in the narratives to follow.

Many and important as are the contradictions, we are not helpless in the disagreement of first-hand witnesses, nor are we compelled to say that, inasmuch as there is such divergent testimony, we must give up all hope of knowing the truth. We shall assemble the evidence; we shall do the careful and necessary work of analysis and synthesis, and shall discover whether we can not make a connected narrative of the part which Abraham Lincoln performed at Gettysburg.

Nearly, if not quite every one who heard the Gettysburg Address and had anything to tell about it worth hearing has now been heard from. The vast majority of those who were present when Lincoln spoke are no longer living. Many of them told their story while they were alive; those who neglected to do this will never tell it to us. The evidence is practically all in. We are able now to assemble it all, to select all that appears to be significant, and to tell the whole story of Lincoln's speech at Gettysburg.

FOREWORD

I acknowledge with deep appreciation the courtesy of the owners of the several Lincoln manuscripts for permission to use them in this book; and my debt to the Library of Congress, already large, is measurably increased. I have special pleasure in acknowledging the many courtesies of Elsie Singmaster, whose assistance has been generous and abundant. Several years ago I explored with her the battle-field of Gettysburg and profited then and later by her correspondence. And last of all, on November 19, 1929, the sixty-sixth anniversary of Lincoln's address, I drove over the battle-field with her, and made the final corrections in the proof-sheets of this volume, with her assistance, where the battle was fought and where Lincoln uttered his immortal words.

WILLIAM E. BARTON

The Lincoln Room,
Pine Knoll on Sunset Lake,
Foxboro, Massachusetts.

CONTENTS

CONTENTS—*Continued*

ILLUSTRATIONS

LINCOLN AT GETTYSBURG

LINCOLN AT GETTYSBURG

CHAPTER I

HOW LINCOLN LEARNED ABOUT GETTYSBURG

THE clock in the War Department struck twelve, and announced the birth of the fourth day of July, in the year of our Lord, 1863. If there was any comment on the fact, or any remark concerning its possible significance, no one remembered it afterward. The anxious group of men who had been sitting through the long and humid hours had passed the point where any one cared to talk or to hear others talk. Edwin M. Stanton had grown tense and irritable. William H. Seward was visibly nervous. Abraham Lincoln sat in a chair tipped back, his tall hat pulled forward to shade his eyes, and was sunk in moody silence. If anything had reminded him of a story, which fortunately nothing did, Stanton or Seward or both would have left the room. One man had already left, and no one had missed him; yet soon all present had occasion to remember that he had been there. He had a right to be there, and if he grew weary of waiting and withdrew, that, also, was his privilege; but no one cared that night whether the Secretary of the Navy remained or went. Gideon Welles was a rather unimportant Connecticut editor when the war broke out, and Lincoln wanted in his Cabinet a man from New England, and other things being equal he preferred a Democrat. So Gideon Welles became a member of the Cabinet.

19

But neither Stanton nor Seward paid much attention to him
or his opinions. He was in the War Department with the
others that night till half past eleven, and when he took his
leave no one noticed his departure. For that matter, no
one cared much for anything except news, and that was
dreaded.

Seldom had official Washington been more sadly eager
for news. General Grant had been pounding away at
Vicksburg, and as far as any one in Washington knew, his
pounding had been ineffectual. The Washington newspapers of July third had printed news which came by way of
Richmond to the effect that Grant had been defeated again.
Nobody imagined that Grant would accept defeat as finality, but on July 3, 1863, no one knew, as the whole country
learned afterward, how many defeats General Grant was
capable of accepting without acknowledging that he was defeated. At midnight of July 3-4, 1863, there was no news
from Vicksburg to cheer the waiting group.

There was another quarter from which information was
eagerly desired. Late in June, General Robert E. Lee and
his Army of Northern Virginia had crossed the Potomac
and passed through Maryland into Pennsylvania. Any
hope of stopping him before he captured Harrisburg
seemed remote. What he would do next was a matter of
conjecture. Between him and Washington was Harper's
Ferry, well garrisoned and at that time the main reliance
depended upon to save the national Capital in case Lee
should turn in that direction. But perhaps he would not
turn that way. He might capture Philadelphia instead, and
then New York; or he might choose to push through to
Lake Erie, cutting all the lines of railroad between the East
and West, and establishing a base of supplies at Buffalo or
Cleveland. He had repeatedly defeated General McClellan. At Fredericksburg, on December 13, 1862, he had

dealt a crushing blow to General Burnside. In the first three days of May, 1863, he had routed the army of General Hooker at Chancellorsville. Hooker had resigned to save himself the necessity of being dismissed, and General George G. Meade had been appointed in his stead as the Commanding General of the Army of the Potomac. Hooker's army had crossed the Potomac in pursuit of Lee, and Meade, succeeding Hooker, had followed Lee into the southern edge of Pennsylvania. For three days there had been vague rumors of a series of terrible battles. Washington had practically no official knowledge and certainly no accurate information with regard to them. The War Department knew nothing except what appeared in the Washington papers, and that was obtained from the newspapers either of Philadelphia or of New York. The evening papers of Friday, July third, reported that Meade had won a great victory, but it was quite certain that this report was not based on any accurate information. With faint hope and deep anxiety, Abraham Lincoln, Secretaries Seward and Stanton, and a little group of others waited until midnight for tidings which did not come. But just as the clock struck twelve, the telegraph instrument clicked.

The message came from Hanover, Pennsylvania, and was addressed, not to Secretary Stanton, nor yet to General Halleck, nor to President Lincoln. For no reason that any one could conjecture, it was directed to the Secretary of the Navy. Stanton pounced upon it without looking around to see whether the man to whom it was addressed was there or not, and having read it, he handed it to the President.

It announced that the sender of the message had been within sight and hearing of a battle fought that day at or near Gettysburg; that he had left the field at half past six in the evening, and that at that hour everything looked hopeful. The dispatch was signed "Byington."

Who was Byington? Everybody asked everybody else and nobody knew. The President directed that a message be wired back at once to Hanover, inquiring "Who is Byington?" The answer came back immediately, "Ask the Secretary of the Navy." Then for the first time they looked around and noticed that the Secretary of the Navy was missing.

Instantly a messenger was dispatched to the home of Secretary Gideon Welles with instructions to get him out of bed and bring him back to the War Department. The President and his companions waited an impatient half-hour for his arrival, and when he got there they thrust into his hands the message, and demanded, "Who is Byington?"

Secretary Welles replied, "Byington is the editor and proprietor of a weekly paper in Norwalk, Connecticut. He sometimes is employed by the New York *Tribune*. Doubtless that newspaper has sent him to report the battle. He is an active and stirring man, and is reliable. The telegram may be depended upon."

Welles went home and went back to bed. He was very proud of the fact that the message had come addressed to him, and that he had been found necessary, like Daniel in the olden time, to interpret the vision. It was the best news that Washington had had about Gettysburg, and nothing more was likely to come or did come that night.

Between one and two o'clock, President Lincoln walked back to the White House. A light rain was beginning to fall, and it was something to be thankful for. The days had been hot and dusty, and the nights were feverish and close. A summer rain was more welcome than anything else could have been except one; that would have been good tidings from one or the other of the two armies just then engaged in mortal combat.

As Lincoln walked home through the cloudy night

lighted up now and then by glows of heat lightning and with muttering thunder in the distance, he must have considered that this was an ominous and unsatisfactory beginning of a Fourth of July celebration, and one very different from such as he would most have enjoyed. The country of which he was President had begun its existence as a nation somewhat longer than eighty years before. He had not computed so as to recall exactly how long it had been, but it was somewhere between eighty and ninety years. How many years longer could a government last that was organized on the basis of human equality before the law? Was this government of which he was the head to have a new birth of liberty, or was it even then in its death agony, doubly stabbed to the heart by the defeat of Grant's army at Vicksburg and the victory of Lee at Gettysburg?

The night grew cool, and it is to be hoped that the anxious President had a few hours of rest before the sultry dawn. No added news came in the morning, but about ten o'clock there were tidings of a semi-official sort which tended to confirm the word received from Byington. At ten-thirty, on the morning of July fourth, the President issued a statement to the country to the effect that "news from the Army of the Potomac up to 10 P. M. of the 3rd, is such as to cover that army with the highest honor; to promise a great success to the cause of the Union, and to claim the condolence of all for the many gallant fallen." He recommended that, on that national anniversary, God should be everywhere remembered and revered with profound gratitude. It was all that he could say, for as yet he had no official news of a decisive sort. It was mildly encouraging.

Two hours later, General Meade telegraphed again. His army was holding Gettysburg, and the enemy had abandoned large numbers of killed and wounded. It was still an inconclusive message, but as far as it went it was encouraging. The day had begun with grave uncertainty; it was still uncertain what the next tidings would be; but the situation had improved at Gettysburg, and if the news from General Grant was not bad, and no disaster occurred to Meade that day or the next, Lincoln could thank God and take courage.

General Meade had won a great victory and did not know it.

CHAPTER II

"Eighty-Odd Years Since"

For the first time in his life little Tad Lincoln shot his firecrackers alone. His brother Willie had died in the winter previous, and Tad was the only boy left in the White House. As for Tad's father, he was too heavily burdened with anxiety to indulge in much festivity. He waited for further news from Meade and from Grant, but he got very little from either quarter. There was enough good news to justify mild rejoicing, but nothing that could warrant a tumultuous celebration. It was a subdued Fourth of July, with one little lonely boy half-heartedly shooting firecrackers on the White House lawn, and a still more lonely President listening with one ear open toward Gettysburg and the other toward Vicksburg, and hearing nothing important in either direction.

It was a fair day in Washington, but in Gettysburg there was heavy rainfall which continued all that day and the next. General Meade was waiting in very great anxiety lest Lee should attack him again. Lee, however, was moving his wagon-trains and his army toward the Potomac, toiling through mud axle-deep in a desperate effort to escape.

All day Sunday Abraham Lincoln waited, and practically speaking he still had no news. No news was good news however; not even Richmond accused General Grant of having lost another battle. No disconcerting tidings from Pennsylvania announced that Lee had recovered from

25

his repulse and was successfully attacking Meade. General Meade was doubtfully considering whether his army could maintain itself through another day's fight. There was one man who knew whether he could do so or not, and that was Robert E. Lee. He was making the best possible use of the stormy weather and the uncertainty in the mind of the Commanding General of the Union Army, and was wading through mud and rain toward the rapidly swelling river that separated him from the Southland. He had risked everything on this invasion of Pennsylvania; if he could only have succeeded, he might have compelled a recognition of the Confederate States by France and Great Britain; but he had lost, and lost hopelessly. If now he should be overtaken as his wearied and bleeding soldiers toiled through the mud, his army would be annihilated. Meade did not know that, but Lee did.

Monday morning came, and the War Department had no authentic news beyond that which was contained in the daily papers, and the Washington papers had no exclusive or important information. All the leading papers, however, were aware by that time that Lee had suffered a terrible defeat. Some of them knew that the series of battles had been the most desperate of the war. To them it appeared that the position of the Confederate Army was now an utterly hopeless one. It was too badly beaten to renew the fight, and if Lee attempted to retreat, he had a swollen river before him, and a victorious army behind. There seemed to be no doubt in anybody's mind that General Lee would be captured or crushed before he got out of Pennsylvania. Washington took on new hope; Lincoln began to smile a pathetic smile shadowed with memories of the brave men who had fallen, but thankful for the victory which seemed to bring the end of the war very near. Still there was no news from General Grant; not until Tuesday did tidings

Photo by W. H. Tipton

The Wills house at Gettysburg, where Lincoln wrote the Address

come from him; but anxiety for Grant was forgotten for the moment in the joy of the victory at Gettysburg.

On the morning of Tuesday, Secretary Edwin M. Stanton wired to his relatives and personal friends, "We have official news this morning that Vicksburg surrendered on the 4th of July." That meant that Pemberton's army had been captured. It meant that dogged, patient, quiet General Grant had not been lost in the swamps about Vicksburg, and that his army, though suffering h avy losses, had pressed steadily forward toward one objective, and had achieved it. That meant, as Lincoln later said, that the Great Father of Waters was to flow unvexed to the sea. It meant that the Confederacy had been cut in twain along the Mississippi. It meant to Abraham Lincoln that there was one General who did not constantly demand of him more soldiers than he could send, but took the army that he had and kept steadily at work until he won a victory. Abraham Lincoln thanked God for General Grant, and had increasing reason to be thankful for him afterward.

On the same day, Tuesday, July seventh, came fuller and more accurate knowledge of the extent of the success at Gettysburg. Not even General Meade had any longer a doubt that he had won a victory. His armies held Gettysburg and all the region roundabout. General Lee was in full retreat, and it was not yet known that his army would be permitted to escape. Lincoln could not believe on that day that Lee could possibly get away. He confidently expected that Lee's army, like Pemberton's, would be captured or destroyed. That Tuesday was the happiest day Lincoln had in all that anxious summer.

On that night Washington formed a procession and, headed by a brass band, marched to the White House. The people had come to serenade the President and congratulate him on two great victories. Abraham Lincoln had been the readiest of stump speakers, but after his election to the presidency he became so extremely careful of his utterances that he was unwilling even to respond to a serenade without having time to write his response. Such time was denied him on that day, and he had to speak as best he could. He had not even found time to subtract 1776 from 1863, but his mind recurred to a thought that had been with him ever since that midnight as he was walking away from the War Department; namely, that it would be a glorious thing if the victory that was to decide the war, or the two victories which together might bring it to an end, could occur or be announced on the nation's birthday. The fourth of July was in the forefront of his thought when he stepped to the White House window to acknowledge the courtesy of the band and thank the people who had accompanied it. He rejoiced with them and thanked God for that which had brought them to the White House on that night. He reminded them that the events which had brought them there had occurred three days before, on the fourth of July. On that day, as he said to them, "for the first time in the history of the world, a nation by its representatives assembled, declared as a self-evident truth that all men are created equal." The battles of that day, he felt sure, had gone some distance toward reaffirming that basic truth of the Declaration of Independence. Just how long ago had it been that all this happened he did not trust himself to say, nor had he time to make the subtraction, as he stood there delivering his little speech; it was "eighty-odd years since, on the fourth of July." Later, he was to compute the interval accurately and state it in a sonorous phrase, "Fourscore and seven years ago." That night he did not remember just how many years it had been, but already he had begun to prepare his Gettysburg Address.

This is what he said:

"Fellow Citizens: I am very glad indeed to see you tonight, and yet I will not say I thank you for this call; but I do most sincerely thank Almighty God for the occasion on which you have called. How long ago is it? Eighty-odd years since, on the fourth of July, for the first time in the history of the world, a nation, by its representatives assembled, declared as a self-evident truth that all men are created equal. That was the birthday of the United States of America. Since then the fourth of July has had several very peculiar recognitions. The two men most distinguished in the framing and support of the Declaration were Thomas Jefferson and John Adams—the one having penned it, and the other sustained it the most forcibly in debate—the only two of the fifty-five who signed it, and were elected Presidents of the United States. Precisely fifty years after they put their hands to the paper, it pleased Almighty God to take both from this stage of action. This was, indeed, an extraordinary and remarkable event in our history. Another President, five years after, was called from this stage of existence on the same day and month of the year; and now on this last fourth of July, just passed, when we have a gigantic rebellion, at the bottom of which is an effort to overthrow the principle that all men were created equal, we have the surrender of a most powerful position and army on that very day. And not only so, but in a succession of battles in Pennsylvania, near to us, through three days, so rapidly fought that they might be called one great battle, on the first, second, and third of the month of July; and on the fourth, the cohorts of those who opposed the declaration that all men are created equal, 'turned tail' and run. [Long continued cheers.] Gentlemen, this is a glorious theme, and the occasion for a speech, but I am not prepared to make one worthy of the occasion. I would like to speak in terms of praise due to the many brave officers and soldiers, who have fought in the cause of the Union and the liberties of their country from the beginning of the war. These are trying occasions, not only in success, but for the want of success. I dislike to mention the name of one single officer, lest I might do wrong to those I might forget. Recent events bring up glorious names, and particularly prominent ones; but these I will not mention. Having said this much, I will now take the music."

The band played again, and the people cheered and went home. It was Lincoln's belated celebration of a truly glorious fourth.

CHAPTER III

THE SORROWFUL SUMMER OF 'SIXTY-THREE

TIDINGS of the two decisive victories sent Abraham Lincoln to bed a happy man on the night of Tuesday, the seventh day of July, 1863. The music of the band had been most welcome. The cheers of the Washington people were pleasant to hear; Washington does not always cheer its presidents. It seemed to Lincoln that the end of the war must be very near. He was too cautious a man to boast about it, but what else was possible? The Confederacy had now no foot to stand on west of the Mississippi; there were Confederate fighting men there, to be sure, but they were cut off from their seat of government and from cooperation with the main bodies of Confederate troops. There was not much now to fear from that quarter. As for Lee, Meade had him at his mercy. Lee was shut in by the swollen flood of the Potomac, and Meade was in position to descend upon him from flank and rear and capture his baggage-trains and utterly rout and destroy his host. The War Department was urging Meade to lose no time in this matter, and the President could not doubt that these urgent orders would be effective.

But Wednesday dawned and died, and Meade did not move. Thursday came and went, and Lee was getting his heavy baggage-trains nearer and nearer the river, and there was no attempt to follow him. Friday arrived and departed, and still Meade, deaf to all orders and appeals, was letting Lee reach the river.

On Saturday, July eleventh, Lincoln was in fine good humor. He had what he accepted as assurance that Meade was about to move and attack Lee. Further, he had word that the Potomac River was so swollen that Lee could not possibly get his army across. Eagerly Lincoln waited for news, but the day and the week ended and the news of Meade's attack did not come.

The same was true on Sunday. Meade's promised attack, if indeed he had promised it, did not occur. Meade wired that he was scouting to find the weak point in Lee's army. Also, he called a council of war. It is an adage among soldiers that a council of war never fights. In every council there are enough cautious men to advise against hazarding the gains that have been won by any rash venturing. Meade did not fight. There is a further adage that a victorious army has its choice in offering to the vanquished a wall of steel or a bridge of gold. Meade offered the bridge of gold. He was more than willing that Lee should escape without the necessity of another battle. Day by day Lincoln fretted and worried; almost every hour some message went from Washington to Meade urging him to fight. Sunday the twelfth, was a rainy day. The President looked out of the window into unrelieved gloom. Monday he was very impatient over Meade's silence. Tuesday, he was profoundly depressed; he had heard from Meade, but his dispatches were timidly worded. At length he had what seemed to indicate that Meade was ready to fight. At noon, on Tuesday, July fourteenth, he received the final message, comforting to Meade but agonizing to the President. Lee had escaped across the Potomac. Meade had "driven the invader from our soil." Lincoln cried, "We had them in our grasp and he let them go! When will our Generals ever get over the idea that an army south of the Potomac has been driven from our soil? The whole country is our soil!"

Lincoln did not stop with words like these. He said that after such a defeat as Lee had suffered at Gettysburg, almost any general could have defeated him. "If I had gone up there, I could have whipped him myself," he said.

Furthermore, the newspapers that told of the escape of Lee told also of the outbreak of the draft riot in New York. Negroes were lynched, and a negro orphan asylum was burned. The *Tribune* office was attacked, and hostile demonstrations were made against various men who were known to be in sympathy with the administration. White men were getting tired of being butchered for the sake of black men who did not appreciate, much less deserve, the sacrifice. Such things and worse the newspapers were saying at the time when Lee, unhindered by Meade, made good his escape across the Potomac. Lincoln was almost furious. "I would give much to be free from the conviction that he was glad to have Lee escape," said Lincoln bitterly. And Meade's announcement of Lee's safe transit was such an expression of relief as to justify Lincoln in that conviction.

If Abraham Lincoln could have known what we know now, that the failure of General Lee to penetrate the North, and the fall of the last fortress that guarded the Mississippi, meant together the inevitable doom of the Confederate Government, the summer of 1863 might have been for him one of comparative comfort. He was, however, too near to the situation to see the outcome of the war as we now see it in perspective. If the rebellion was to be put down, Lincoln must have more soldiers. The South could maintain itself, and did, for months and months after the fall of Vicksburg and the defeat at Gettysburg. Every battle cost the South a heavy loss, but the South, fighting on inside lines, could hold the front with a much smaller number of troops than the North. Lincoln must have more soldiers. Proclamations ceased to bring them. No longer did they come singing in happy anticipation of an easy victory, "We are coming Father Abraham, three hundred thousand strong." In 1862 there had been a draft. It was far from being a complete success. The states were very slow in accepting their quotas and slower still in filling them. Other drafts followed in 1863, and they were more rigorous than those of the preceding year. They provoked not simply opposition, but in some places armed resistance. In Indiana and the states adjacent, a secret society known as the Knights of the Golden Circle sprang up to furnish aid and sympathy to the southern cause, and to resist the draft.

Three hundred dollars would buy an exemption, and thousands of men prepared to save that amount of money in case they should be drawn. The highly profitable business of bounty-jumping came into existence. A respectable citizen, having been drawn, would pay three hundred dollars to some worthless fellow to enlist in his stead, or a town that was behind in its quota of soldiers would pay twice or thrice that sum for a volunteer to be credited to its quota. The new recruits secured under these conditions would often pocket the money, desert and sell their services to other men or other towns.

Lincoln did not know it, but in the South conditions were even worse. The whole Southland was drained of its young manhood. Patriotism no longer filled the gaps which the battles had torn in the armies of Lee and his associates. The laws governing enlistments were carefully studied, and every form of exemption was worked to its utter limit. In the South, school-teachers were exempted from military service, provided they could show that they were actually engaged in the instruction of not less than twenty pupils each. A great hunger for education took possession of the South. Every man who could secure twenty more or less qualified pupils registered as a teacher, no matter how little he knew about books or learning. Jefferson Davis was harder driven for new soldiers than was Abraham Lincoln, but Lincoln had a sorrowful time of it.

Lincoln was very desirous that east Tennessee should be captured from the Confederacy, and that its people, mainly loyal, should have an opportunity to manifest their fidelity to the Union. General Burnside was sent to Knoxville, but there he was hemmed in by Longstreet and almost lost his army. Lincoln grew very solicitous about him. It was a rather good day when they had no news from Knoxville, and when now and then word came that there was fighting in that vicinity, Lincoln comforted himself by remembering how Sally Carter, when she heard one of her children crying, was accustomed to say, "That's one of my young ones; not dead yet, thank the Lord!" But the fact that Burnside was not dead, and his army not obliterated, did not indicate any very rapid progress toward the deliverance of east Tennessee.

All summer long General Rosecrans had been practically inactive. He had captured Murfreesboro in the past winter, and late in June by a series of really brilliant maneuvers he forced the Confederates out of middle Tennessee and back to the Tennessee River at Chattanooga. Lincoln was very eager that this city should be captured, for it was an important rail and river center, but Rosecrans delayed anything like an aggressive movement. On September nineteenth, he fought a bloody battle at Chickamauga. There it seemed his army would have been hopelessly defeated but for the tenacity of General Thomas, who, though not a brilliant general, was brave and reliable. The manner in which Thomas held his line, and so saved the army, entitled him to the name he won, the "Rock of Chickamauga." The battles of Missionary Ridge and Lookout Mountain remained to be fought. Rosecrans and

Bragg faced each other in the vicinity of Chattanooga, and Lincoln was looking forward with great solicitude to the fight that must occur there.

As for General Lee, his army was not in condition to undertake any marked aggressive movement, and General Meade was not disposed to push him. The summer went on with far less to cheer the lonely man in the White House than he or we could have wished.

Meanwhile the political pot was boiling. In the summer of 1863, the United States of America had no intention of reelecting Abraham Lincoln as President of the United States. That he had done about as well under all the circumstances as could reasonably have been expected of him, was as charitable a judgment as almost any one at that time cared to pass upon him. Any general who could have fought so brilliant a battle in 1863 as to have brought the Civil War to an end by the summer of 1864 could have had the presidential nomination of either party in the autumn of that year. This was the consideration which had forced Lincoln largely against his judgment to appoint General Joseph H. Hooker Commander-in-Chief of the Army of the Potomac after the failure of Burnside at Fredericksburg. Hooker, as Lincoln knew and said, did not mix politics with his fighting. That was why Salmon P. Chase and his friends were insistent that Hooker be placed in command of the Army of the Potomac. If he had won instead of losing at Chancellorsville, and then by brilliant battles had forced Lee into Richmond and at length compelled the surrender of that city, and thus had ended the war during the winter of 1863-64, the prestige of his victories would have gone far toward making Salmon P. Chase President. General Joseph H. Hooker knew to what influences he owed his appointment, and he not only sent his reports to the War Department but he furnished duplicates to Secretary Chase. Furthermore, the abolitionists, dissatisfied with Lincoln because he had been so slow in issuing the Emancipation Proclamation, were now seeking a more pronounced abolitionist as his successor.

These were some of the reasons why the summer of 1863 was not wholly a comfortable time for Abraham Lincoln. The significance of the victory at Gettysburg bulked larger as the months went by. The importance of the opening of the Mississippi was increasingly apparent. The prospect that foreign nations would recognize the Confederate Government grew more remote. The advantages were increasingly on the side of the North. The year 1863 was a better year for the Federal Government than 1862, but it gave to the sad man in the White House far less than its legitimate comfort.

One matter, however, of considerable importance grew out of Lincoln's meditation on that summer. He made mental note of the two Generals who simultaneously had won notable victories. He forced himself to believe that General Meade had, on the whole, done fairly well. Meade continued in command of the Army of the Potomac, but Lincoln was not disposed to accord him larger responsibility. Lincoln looked with increasing interest farther west, and noted the dogged determination with which a quiet man from his own state maintained his record for persistent fighting and held with pertinacity to all his gains. After a while he appointed Ulysses S. Grant, Commander-in-Chief of all the army, and with a sigh of relief, he said, "I don't know General Grant's plans, and I don't intend to ask him. Thank God, I have found a General."

CHAPTER IV

Lincoln Decides to Visit Gettysburg

THE war was not won at Gettysburg; it was won in the West. At the end of 1864, General Grant was little nearer Richmond than General McClellan had been in 1862. The victories of Grant at Shiloh, Vicksburg and Chattanooga, of Thomas at Franklin and Nashville, and of Sherman on his march to the sea, not only inflicted on the Confederate armies irreparable losses, but steadily diminished the area under control of the southern government and left it with no hope of regaining its lost ground. With the whole region west of the Mississippi lost, and with the active operations of Lee's army confined to the eastern part of Virginia, with ineffective resistance in a few detached areas, the last stage of the Civil War was that in which General Grant adopted, and tenaciously held, a stern policy of wearing out the Confederate Army by slow but remorseless attrition. The war ended far from the places in which it was won, and some time afterward, but it ended as Gettysburg ended, in a victory for the Union. It had not ended and the end was not in sight when Lincoln went to Gettysburg.

Lincoln was troubled about the political situation. The Democratic party was certain to choose as its nominee the disgruntled and discredited General George B. McClellan. His followers would say, and did say, that Lincoln had failed to give him the support he needed, and removed him from office for political reasons. They were certain to make a great many voters believe that this was true. Large

38

numbers of the abolitionists were not disposed to give Lincoln much credit for having freed the slaves. Secretary Seward protested to the artist, Frank B. Carpenter, over his choice of the reading of the Emancipation Proclamation as the incident to be painted in his life-sized canvas of the President and his Cabinet. Seward said that the freeing of the slaves was the direct and inevitable result of the organization of the Republican party, and no one incident of the Lincoln administration was of marked significance in connection with it. Abolitionists far more extreme than Seward were organizing to nominate, and did nominate, General John C. Frémont for the presidency. Lincoln said of Frémont that he was like Jim Jett's little brother, of whom Jim said that he was the greatest rascal on earth, but by the mercy of divine Providence was kept from doing the harm that might have been expected of him because he was also the greatest fool. Most irritating of all the opposition to Lincoln was the open and undenied candidacy of Honorable Salmon P. Chase, Lincoln's Secretary of the Treasury. He never believed that Lincoln was a great man, and had no doubt that between 1861 and 1864 the nation would discover its mistake and elect Salmon P. Chase as his successor. Chase had large correspondence, and his letters from prominent men, declaring that the country must avoid the mistake on the one hand of reelecting Lincoln and on the other of choosing a military President, were sweet music in his ears. He felt confident that his own state of Ohio would support him, and he hoped that the prospective marriage of his brilliant daughter, Kate, to Governor Sprague, of Rhode Island, would give him also the support of New England. Lincoln knew of Chase's movements, and said that they were in bad taste, but if they succeeded he could only hope the country might never have a worse President than Chase would make. But, like the bluebottle fly, Chase, as Lincoln said, was laying his eggs in every rotten spot he could find, and it was far from being impossible that he might succeed.

Considering how ambitious he was, Abraham Lincoln did singularly little consciously to promote his second election. Not only in 1863 but late in the summer of 1864, he really believed that he could not be reelected; and he made a solemn and silent but recorded pledge that in the event of his defeat he would help his successor to win the war before the inauguration, for he was sure the winning of it would be impossible afterward.

Still, there were cheering events. On August 7, 1863, John Hay wrote in his diary:

"The Tycoon is in fine whack. I have rarely seen him more serene and busy. He is managing this war, the draft, foreign relations, and planning a reconstruction of the Union all at once. I never knew with what tyrannous authority he rules the Cabinet till now. The most important things he decides and there is no comment. I am growing more and more convinced that the good of the country demands that he should be kept where he is till this thing is over. There is no man in the country so gritty and firm. I believe the hand of God placed him where he is. They are all working against him like braves, though, but don't seem to make anything by it. I believe the people know what they want, and unless politics have grown in power and lost in principle, they will have it."

Again on September 11, 1863, Hay wrote to Nicolay, then temporarily away from Washington:

"You may talk as you please of the abolition Cabinet directing affairs from Washington; some well-meaning newspapers advise the President to keep his fingers out of the military pie, and all that sort of thing. The truth is, if he did, the pie would be a sorry mess. The old man sits here and wields like a backwoods Jupiter the bolts of war and the machinery of government with a hand equally steady and equally firm."

In some respects Lincoln's worst fears were realized. Meade lost no battles, neither did he win any. Burnside was badly out-generaled by Longstreet at Knoxville. As for Rosecrans, he lost Chickamauga and lost his nerve, and had to be removed. But Grant succeeded him, and Lincoln believed in Grant.

Lincoln understood and approved Grant's simple plan of putting into action at one time the largest possible force, and on the largest number of fronts, thus forbidding the advantage the Confederates had on inside lines of moving their reserves from one spot to another. And that was the costly but effective policy that won the war.

Abraham Lincoln kept thinking about Gettysburg. If only the war could have been finished there! What a saving of blood and treasure if the victory had been followed up! He could scarcely bring himself to believe that Meade's cautious policy had been justified. He kept thinking that if he himself had been there, in command of the army, he would have ended the war then and there. "I could have whipped Lee myself," he kept saying to himself. He was careful not to say it to any of his generals, but he did more than say it to himself. He said it where Robert Lincoln overheard it, and Robert told John Hay. "I knew he had that idea," said John.

Lincoln wanted to see Gettysburg with his own eyes, and discover if the situation was not as he thought. There was no use crying over spilled milk. There were other and immediate matters to worry about. And there was much to be thankful for. Meade's victory had been very different from McClellan's at Antietam, and Meade had more excuse. He had no little reason to be cautious after all that had happened. Lincoln wrote Meade a letter filled with expressions of bitter disappointment, and decided not to mail it. It was too late to help matters now, and it might wound the spirit of a brave and loyal soldier. But Lincoln kept thinking about Gettysburg, and wishing that he could see it for himself.

CHAPTER V

The Cemetery

General Lee withdrew from Gettysburg, leaving behind him twenty-five hundred Confederate dead; more than that number of dead Union soldiers lay with them in the rain. Besides these, there were more than twenty thousand wounded. The churches, the Theological Seminary and a number of barns were used as hospitals. Many soldiers died each day. The first duty was the rescue and care of the wounded. After that came the burial of the dead.

Such burial as appeared immediately practicable was of a very superficial character. Those soldiers who died in battle were covered where they fell. Those who died in hospitals were hastily buried in the nearest convenient spot. In a majority of cases no grave was dug; a meager covering of earth was spaded over the body; how meager it was, the next rain disclosed.

At that time the National Government had made no provision for cemeteries to be owned by the government for the burial of soldiers of the Civil War. Scores of thousands of Union soldiers lay in graves in the Southland, and a much smaller number of bodies, claimed by relatives, had been shipped to their homes from various battle-fields. Such neglect as there had been had seemed inevitable in the stress of circumstances.

The geographical location of Gettysburg suggested a different plan. The Union soldiers who died there, fell, not

43

in the Southland, but in a populous northern state, and their place of burial was within convenient access of the great eastern cities.

Governor Andrew G. Curtin, of Pennsylvania, appointed a local agent as his representative in looking after the wounded in and about Gettysburg. He was David Wills, a public-spirited citizen, later a judge. Mr. Wills made reports to the Governor, and later to the Legislature, and submitted a series of recommendations whose wisdom is now clearly apparent.

The people of Gettysburg were agreed that conditions as they existed in midsummer, 1863, were intolerable. The Union dead ought to be gathered from their places of temporary interment into one convenient spot. The managers of the local cemetery association were the first to suggest a plan. It was that the Union dead should be buried in an annex to the village cemetery, under the management of the local corporation. This suggestion was not without the hope that thus by the sale of so many burial plots the treasury of the local cemetery association would prosper.

A communication from Mr. Wills says:

"A persistent effort was made by persons here, to have the soldiers buried in grounds controlled by the local cemetery association of this place. The plan proposed having the burials made at a stipulated price, to be paid to the cemetery association. Failing in this project, these persons endeavored to connect the two cemeteries, so that they should be in one inclosure, and all under the control, supervision and management of the local cemetery association."

Mr. Wills strongly opposed this plan, and so did Governor Curtin, who visited the village soon after the battle. A radically different plan was proposed. Under the general statutes of Pennsylvania, as under those of other states, it was possible to create a corporation, not for financial profit, organized for the purpose of establishing and maintaining cemeteries. This general statute was deemed adequate, and a special corporation was created known as "The National Soldiers' Cemetery." The plan was that a body of trustees or commissioners should be formed, one member appointed by each northern governor whose state had lost men at Gettysburg. The corporation thus formed should be legally authorized to own and manage a cemetery free from local control.

In anticipation of such organization, Mr. Wills, acting under authority from Governor Curtin, purchased in the name of the state of Pennsylvania, a plot of land on the Baltimore turnpike which had been the apex of the triangular line of the Union defense, the point where the Louisiana Tigers had been repelled on Thursday evening. The whole original purchase was about seventeen acres. Governor Curtin approved this plan, and Mr. Wills moved with commendable promptness. The Governors of other states were cordial in their approval and cooperation. The cost of the grounds, the improvements and the burials, was apportioned among the states, not in the proportion of their soldiers buried at Gettysburg, but in the ratio of their congressional representation. To the two large states of Pennsylvania and New York, both of which had large numbers of soldiers in the fight, the plan made little difference, but Illinois, that had only six soldiers buried in Gettysburg, paid twelve thousand dollars, while Massachusetts, with one hundred and fifty-eight of her soldiers buried there, paid but two-thirds as much. There appears to have been no bickering or dissent. The plan was accepted as just, and was adhered to without objection. The states all met the apportionments which their Governors had accepted. The

legal details required several months, but the soil in which
the Union dead of Gettysburg were to be buried was held
by representatives appointed by the Governors of their own
states.   These were eighteen in number: Maine, New
Hampshire, Vermont, Massachusetts, Rhode Island, Connecticut, New York, New Jersey, Pennsylvania, Delaware,
Maryland, West Virginia, Ohio, Indiana, Illinois, Michi-
gan, Wisconsin and Minnesota.

Gettysburg had an unusual amount of sickness that
autumn, and it was believed that it resulted in part at least
from the shallow burials.   The removal of bodies began
late in October, but was stopped until after frost.   The
records do not show how many bodies had been removed
to the new location at the time of the dedication, but it was
no large fraction of the whole number.

The cemetery was laid out in a half-circle, with a central
space reserved for an imposing monument.   This monument was later erected by the National Government at a
cost of fifty thousand dollars.   It stands where the speakers' platform was erected at the time of the dedication.

The work of removal and reinterment of bodies under
the contract began Tuesday, October 27, 1863, and was
completed March 18, 1864.   The total number of reinter-
ments at that time numbered 3512, of whom all but 979
were identified.

Bodies in considerable numbers were discovered after
the contract had been completed.   Indeed, sixty years after
the battle occasional burials continue to be disclosed by the
plow or spade.   A belt-buckle or some buttons usually show
to which army the soldier belonged.   No final figures are
therefore available, for still it occurs now and then that a
new grave is dug at Gettysburg, and a few bones are rein-
terred in the section reserved for the unidentified Union
dead of the battle.

CHAPTER VI

Preparations for the Dedication

As the Gettysburg Cemetery was rescued from becoming a local enterprise, and placed in charge of a corporation which, if not fully national, was at least of interstate character, it was proposed to dedicate the ground with imposing ceremonies. This plan was agreed upon in September, before the removal of the bodies began.

A date, October 23, 1863, was set, and an invitation was issued to Edward Everett, believed to be the foremost orator in America, to deliver the oration. He replied that it would be impossible for him to make adequate preparation in the time proposed. To meet his convenience, the dedication was postponed nearly a month, until Thursday, November nineteenth.

The date being fixed, formal invitations were sent to the President and Cabinet, to General Meade and the venerable General Winfield Scott, to all members of the diplomatic corps, to all members of both Houses of Congress, and to many other distinguished citizens. Few, comparatively, of those invited, accepted. General Meade, smarting under the rebuke of the President for not following Lee, declined, giving as his excuse the army's need of him. General Scott did not attend on account of his age and infirmities.

If the Gettysburg Cemetery had been at the outset what it is now, a tract owned and controlled by the National Government, the President would almost certainly have

47

had a share in the planning of the service of dedication. As it was, he had no official responsibility whatever. The Governors of the several states that had soldiers buried there, and not the President of the nation, controlled that situation, and they were working through the commission, just appointed and beginning its labor. It had not occurred to any one that it was a matter in which the President was likely to have any important concern. Just why he was so much interested, we do not yet know. He never gave a reason for it. That reason could not have been either that the invitation was urgent, or that his was deemed a necessary part of the program.

President Lincoln's invitation to be present at the dedication at Gettysburg was not a written individual request such as had been sent to Edward Everett and others. It did not occur to any member of the commission that such a missive should be addressed to him. What was sent to him was the printed circular of which many hundreds were mailed and was in no respect different from that sent to the most obscure congressman from Minnesota or a consul from Patagonia. The sending of it to the President was a mere formality. When Mr. Wills informed his fellow officials of Mr. Lincoln's acceptance, that group was very greatly surprised, and they can not be said to have been overjoyed.

If Lincoln had been seeking a reason for not attending the exercises at Gettysburg, he had all the excuse he could have desired, and more. Not only was public business pressing, not only was he restlessly desirous of getting under way the message which he had to present to the Congress which was soon to assemble, but there were domestic reasons why he might have decided to remain at home. Little Tad was sick, and no one knew just how sick he was or what was the matter with him. Little Willie had died

Photo by W. H. Tipton

High Water-Mark Monument—scene of Pickett's charge

in February, 1862, and that sorrow had driven Mrs. Lincoln almost insane. When Tad was taken sick, she was filled with anxiety. Tad, the little tongue-tied lad with the cleft palate and the slow intellectual development, was a lovable, spoiled, undisciplined boy. With Bob in Harvard, Tad was all that remained of the young life that at one time had made the Lincoln home a noisy happy place. Tad slept with his father in the White House. His habit was to hang around the office in the evening, running in and out at will, and at length falling asleep there. Then his tall father would throw Tad across his shoulder, doubling him up like a jack-knife, and carry him up to bed, descending after a few minutes to resume the conference or conversation. Tad was not quite so well on the day when Lincoln took his departure for Gettysburg, and Tad's father, to say nothing of Tad's mother, was concerned for him. Nevertheless, he went. He told Edward Everett of his solicitude. Everett inquired about Tad next day, and Lincoln wrote, "Our sick boy, for whom you kindly inquired, we hope is past the worst." Tad was not past the worst when his father left him. The fact that President Lincoln left Tad sick and his mother hysterical shows that he certainly wanted to go.

The President having accepted their invitation to attend, the member of the Board from Illinois proposed that Mr. Lincoln should be invited to make a brief address. Colonel Clark E. Carr, the said member, does not in fact make this statement in his charming and reliable little book on the subject. But Colonel Carr informed his personal friends, among them the author of this volume, that it was he who made the suggestion, and that the proposal was not received with marked enthusiasm by all the members of the commission. Colonel Carr said:

"The proposition to ask Mr. Lincoln to speak at the Gettysburg ceremonies was an afterthought. The President of the United States had, like the other distinguished personages, been invited to be present, but Mr. Lincoln was not, at that time, invited to speak. In fact, it did not seem to occur to any one that he could speak on such an occasion.

"Scarcely any member of the Board, excepting the member representing Illinois, had ever heard him speak at all, and no other member had ever heard, or read from him, anything except political discussions. When the suggestion was made that he be invited to speak, while all expressed high appreciation of his great abilities as a political speaker, as shown in his debate with Stephen A. Douglas, and in his Cooper Institute address, the question was raised as to his ability to speak upon such a grave and solemn occasion as that of the memorial services. Besides, it was said that, with his important duties and responsibilities, he could not possibly have the leisure to prepare an address for such an occasion. In answer to this, it was urged that he himself, better than anyone else, could determine as to these questions, and that, if he were invited to speak, he was sure to do what under the circumstances, would be right and proper.

"It must be remembered that Mr. Lincoln had not proved to the world his ability to speak upon such an occasion. He had not yet made a Gettysburg address, and he had not then made that other great address, which for sublimity and pathos ranks next to it, his second inaugural.

"It was finally decided to ask President Lincoln 'after the oration' (that is to say, after Mr. Everett's oration) as chief executive of the nation, 'to set apart formally these grounds to their sacred use by a few appropriate remarks.' This was done in the name of the Governors of the States, as was the case with others, by Mr. Wills; but the invitation was not settled upon and sent to Mr. Lincoln until the second of November, more than six weeks after Mr. Everett had been invited to speak, and but a little more than two weeks before the exercises were held."*

No wonder people were surprised. Tardy and lacking in enthusiasm as the invitation was, President Lincoln accepted it. He agreed to make the "few appropriate remarks" which his invitation specified.

When it was reported that the President was going to Gettysburg, having hardly been invited, an explanation seemed to many people to be close at hand. For many years there had been a factional fight in Pennsylvania between Andrew G. Curtin, the war Governor of the state, and Simon Cameron, who had succeeded James Buchanan as senator and whom Lincoln had appointed, with many misgivings, Secretary of War. Pennsylvania had not been normally a Republican state, and its vote in 1864 was imperiled by the strife between the two outstanding Republican leaders. In proportion as Lincoln had won favor with the Cameron faction by a Cabinet appointment followed by an ambassadorship to Russia, he had tended to alienate the friends of Curtin. But Lincoln owed much to Curtin, and wanted to retain his enthusiastic support. Except for the strength of Curtin in the Pennsylvania delegation at Chicago in 1860, Lincoln probably could not have been nominated. Of all the loyal Governors, none had stood more strongly behind Lincoln than Andrew G. Curtin, of Pennsylvania. But Simon Cameron still was a man to be reckoned with. His hold on Pennsylvania was so strong that he was four times chosen senator, and he could have had a fifth term of six years if he had not preferred to hand the

*Lincoln at Gettysburg, by Clark E. Carr, pp. 21-25.

nomination over to his son; and that son was senator for term after term. Lincoln must not offend Cameron, and he must win a little more assuredly the support of Curtin before the campaign of 1864 set in. The friends of Curtin were already proclaiming him as the next Republican candidate for Vice-President. Lincoln had no immediate obligation to declare how he stood on that question, but he had some occasion to let it be known that he appreciated Curtin. This Cemetery affair at Gettysburg was Andy Curtin's pet scheme, and it was alleged that it was his strong bid for the soldier vote. Lincoln, by going to Gettysburg, could honor Curtin without offending Cameron.

Lincoln had been trying to settle a factional fight among the Republicans of Missouri, and had got abuse from both sides. Here was his chance to take a hand in the Pennsylvania affair and win political friends without losing any.

So said some of the newspapers. Abraham Lincoln was ready to make a stump-speech over the graves of soldiers for the sake of securing a political advantage. The editors did not doubt that that was the kind of speech he intended to make; and their righteous souls were vexed by reason of his anticipated profanation of that sacred spot.

Such was the ready explanation made by those editors and politicians in 1863, who thought it quite unnecessary to impute a high and noble motive to the President when a mean and contemptible one lay ready to their hand. Lincoln knew of this criticism, and in the face of it, he must have had need of no little courage to go to Gettysburg, when he had so many good excuses for remaining away.

Under all these circumstances, why did Lincoln go to Gettysburg?

Certainly he did not go to make a political speech. Every word and sentence of his address is evidence that such a motive was not in his mind. Perhaps his first impulse to go grew out of the notion he had had from the beginning that he himself could have defeated Lee at Gettysburg, and he wanted to see what Gettysburg was like. Perhaps he wanted to pay his silent tribute of reverence to the brave men who had died there. Perhaps when he was invited to speak he wanted to summon the people there assembled to join him in a new dedication of the whole nation to the unfinished task which they who fought there had thus far so nobly advanced.

I am inclined to believe that one reason Lincoln cared to go to Gettysburg was that he had visited the battle-field of Antietam in the previous autumn, and that visit had become the occasion of a cruel and unworthy report that the President had behaved there with unbecoming levity; and General George B. McClellan, who was in a position to have denied the report, and who by every rule of honor ought to have done so, failed to do it. Lincoln was cut to the heart by that incident, and I think he wanted to go to Gettysburg under conditions that would make another such report impossible, and might afford him opportunity to appear as a simple and silent participant in a service that was to be held in honor of the dead heroes of another and a greater battle.

Whatever his reasons, he determined to go, and later he consented to speak. It was a courageous decision on his part. He risked much in going to Gettysburg. He would have saved himself no little criticism if he had decided at the last minute that he was needed in Washington.

CHAPTER VII

THE JOURNEY

NOT very much was said in Washington about the President's prospective journey to Gettysburg. The members of the Cabinet had received invitations when the President received his, and half of them had declined. The others had not given the matter sufficient attention to reply. Lincoln, however, was giving such thought as he could to the preparation of the "few appropriate remarks" which he was expected to make. But the short November days were slipping away, and the Gettysburg celebration was approaching. There were, however, other matters that had to receive attention.

In August, 1863, Lincoln had sat to Alexander Gardner, the photographer who had succeeded Matthew Brady, and some photographic negatives were made. The day was fine, and the President was in good spirits, but for some reason the pictures were not deemed satisfactory. On Sunday morning, November eighth, Lincoln, accompanied by Nicolay, Hay, Noah Brooks and others, went again to the same photographer and had a number of pictures made, including one of a group, showing the President and his two secretaries. The President had already received the proof-sheets of Edward Everett's address, set up by the Boston *Journal,* and supplied well in advance for the use of the newspapers of the country and for other proper purposes. After he had started for the gallery he turned back to the White House and procured these sheets, covering nearly two full newspaper pages, and during the intervals between exposures, which in those days of wet-plate photography were comparatively long, he read portions of Everett's address. In one or more of the pictures made that day the proof-sheets appear on the table.

One incident in the social life of Washington must not be omitted. It occurred precisely a week before the dedication at Gettysburg, that is to say, on Thursday, November 12, 1863. This was the marriage of Kate, daughter of Honorable Salmon P. Chase, Secretary of the Treasury, to Governor Sprague, of Rhode Island. It was a brilliant party, and the élite of Washington were there. Several generals, among them Schenck, Stoneman and McDowell, were present in uniform. Former Secretary of War, Simon Cameron, of Pennsylvania, was there. President Abraham Lincoln was present for a little while, and then excused himself and went home; Mrs. Lincoln was not attending social functions since the death of Willie, and for that matter the President and his lady were not supposed to attend private functions. This, however, was no ordinary private function. Kate Chase was the most brilliant woman in Washington, and she was marrying to her father's supposed political advantage. Governor Sprague was a man of influence in New England, and he was expected to do much to advance the political fortunes of his new father-in-law. Kate Chase Sprague would see that her husband did not forget. Salmon P. Chase had been one of the most brilliant entertainers in Washington. His bills for wines, all duly receipted and filed, show that guests lacked for nothing at his board. He had entertained with a discriminating lavishness, and had drawn together beneath his roof the men whom he expected to help him to become President.*

---

*The wine-bills of Secretary Chase, with much interesting correspondence relating to his presidential aspirations, are in the Library of Congress.

Abraham Lincoln had that to think about as he walked home from the Chase wedding. Kate Chase had made a match not only of social but of political importance. All the women in Washington said so. But that was not all they said. They declared, or if they did not their husbands did, that her marriage marked a long step in advance for her father.

Kate Chase was married, and to John Hay she looked very tired on her wedding night:

"Kate looked tired out and languid, especially at the close of the evening. When I went to the bridal chamber to say good night, she had lost all her old severity and formal stiffness of manner, and seemed to think she had *arrived.*"

On Tuesday, November seventeenth, the President brought up the matter of the Gettysburg dedication at the Cabinet meeting, and requested Secretary Stanton to arrange for a special train. Stanton agreed to do so, but excused himself from going. Matters about Chattanooga looked too grave for him to be gone. Secretary Welles also excused himself on account of the pressure of official business. Secretaries Seward, Usher and Blair agreed to go. Secretary Chase was not present, and Lincoln sent him a little note:

"My Dear Sir: I expected to see you here at Cabinet meeting, and to say something about going to Gettysburg. There will be a train to take and return us. The time of starting is not yet fixed, but when it shall be I will notify you.

"Yours truly,

"A. Lincoln."

But Honorable Salmon P. Chase had several other matters to think about. He declined to go to Gettysburg on account of the importance of public business. Later in the afternoon, Secretary Stanton sent the following note to the White House:

"Mr. President:

"It is proposed by the Baltimore and Ohio road—

"First, To leave Washington Thursday morning at 6 A. M.; and

"Second, To leave Baltimore at 8 A. M., arriving at Gettysburg at 12 noon, thus giving two hours to view the ground before the dedication services commence.

"Third, To leave Gettysburg at 6 P. M., and arrive in Washington, midnight; thus doing all in one day.

"Mr. Smith says the Northern Central road agrees to this arrangement.

"Please consider it, and if any change is desired, let me know, so that it can be made.

"Yours truly,

"Edwin M. Stanton."

Lincoln did not approve this arrangement. He returned Stanton's time-table with this notation:

"I do not like this arrangement. I do not wish to so go that by the slightest accident we fail entirely; and at the best, the whole to be a mere breathless running of the gauntlet. But any way.

"A. Lincoln."

Stanton made the change. Messages were sent on that evening to the officials concerned, informing them that the train would depart from the Baltimore and Ohio Station at noon of Wednesday, November eighteenth.

Lincoln had a special escort from the War Department, General James B. Fry. The latter called at the White House in a carriage to convey the President to the train. The President was not ready. When General Fry remarked that they would have to hurry to make the train, Lincoln was reminded of the man in Illinois who was being conveyed to the gallows. As spectators were hurrying past his cart, he called out, "Boys, you needn't be in such a hurry; there won't be any fun till I get there."

The party included the President and Secretaries Seward, Usher and Blair; the President's two secretaries, John G. Nicolay and John Hay; M. Mercier, the French Minister, M. Bertinatti, the Italian Minister, and other distinguished guests. There were four cars, the rear coach being a directors' car. The rear third of this car was partitioned off into a kind of drawing-room, and in that the President sat with the more prominent of his fellow-travelers. Other individuals and groups got on at Baltimore and elsewhere along the way. The group inside the drawing-room changed somewhat as men came and went. The President had little time to himself.

At Baltimore, the cars were drawn by horses across to the tracks of the Northern Central Railway, at the Calvert Street Station. When the train was made up again, a baggage-car was added, fitted up as a dining-car for those members of the party who had left Washington without lunch, which number included the President. Most of those who got on at Baltimore had lunched before leaving. At Hanover Junction the train switched over to the Western Maryland tracks.

At each of these stops the President stepped out upon the platform and said a few words to the people who assembled to greet him. At one point a little girl gave him a bouquet. The President bent low and kissed her, saying that she was a "sweet little rose-bud."

The principal conversation of the journey, as far as we have report, was that of the President with Wayne Mac-Veagh, then an important young Pennsylvania attorney, and later Attorney-General of the United States. MacVeagh told John Hay that he had "pitched into" the President for his Missouri policy. Apparently the President did not resent this, for as the train was on its way back to Washington the next night, the President, though very tired and not very well, sent for MacVeagh for a further word.

The journey occupied the entire afternoon. The train reached Gettysburg at dusk. The President was conveyed to the home of Mr. Wills, which fronted on the public square, called the "Diamond." Gettysburg had a hotel, but it was crowded, and better accommodations were to be had at the Wills house. The arrangement proved a comfortable one. There the President and the other guests had supper. Seward and other notable guests were entertained next door in the home of Mr. Harper.

CHAPTER VIII

The Evening at Gettysburg

That was Gettysburg's greatest night. At the time of the battle there was more noise, but the cannon stopped at dusk or before. A number of military bands had come in from different cities, and they went about like roaring lions seeking whom they might serenade.

John Hay and other gay spirits made a festive night of it. They had an oyster supper at the college, other refreshments elsewhere, and went abroad singing *John Brown's Body* and other up-to-date music.

The town was full, and the weather was mild. Not many people cared to go to bed. An excited crowd wanted to enjoy as much music and hear as many eminent men as possible.

A band serenaded the President that evening, and he was called upon for a speech, and, quite unwilling to divide the material of the address he was working on, he said:

"I appear before you, fellow citizens, merely to thank you for this compliment. The inference is a very fair one that you would hear me for a little while at least, were I to commence to make a speech. I do not appear before you for the purpose of doing so, and for several substantial reasons. The most substantial of these is that I have no speech to make. In my position it is sometimes important that I should not say any foolish things. (A voice: If you can help it.) It very often happens that the only way to help it is to say nothing at all. Believing that is my present condition this evening, I must beg of you to excuse me from addressing you further."

That was not a very tactful speech, and it did not please all his hearers. Lincoln was tired, and was burdened with the necessity of speaking the next day.

The crowd went next door, and Secretary Seward was more ready to speak. He made the mistake of assuming that because he was near the Maryland line, his hearers were southerners. Perhaps it would have been as well for him if he also had declined. But he delivered a little address:

"Fellow Citizens:—I am now sixty years old and upwards; I have been in public life practically forty years of that time, and yet this is the first time that ever any people, or community, so near to the border of Maryland, was found willing to listen to my voice; and the reason was that I saw, forty years ago, that slavery was opening before this people a graveyard that was to be filled with brothers falling in mutual political combat. I knew that the cause that was hurrying the Union into this dreadful strife was slavery; and when, during all the intervening period, I elevated my voice, it was to warn the people to remove that cause while they could, by constitutional means, and so avert the catastrophe of civil war which has fallen upon the nation. I am thankful that you are willing to hear me at last. I thank my God that I believe this strife is going to end in the removal of that evil, which ought to have been removed by deliberate councils and peaceful means. (Good.) I thank my God for the hope that this is the last fratricidal war which will fall upon the country which is vouchsafed to us by Heaven,—the richest, the broadest, the most beautiful, the most magnificent, and capable of a great destiny, that has ever been given to any part of the human race. (Applause.) And I thank Him for the hope that when that cause is removed, simply by the operation of abolishing it, as the origin and agent of the treason that is without justification, and without parallel, we shall thenceforth be united, be only one country, having only one hope, one ambition and one destiny. (Applause.) Tomorrow, at least, we shall feel that we are not enemies, but that we are friends and brothers, that this Union is a reality, and we shall mourn together for the evil wrought by this rebellion. We are now near the graves of the misguided, whom we have consigned to their last resting place, with pity for their errors, and with the same heart full of grief with which we mourn over a brother by whose hand, raised in defence of his government, that misguided brother perished.

"When we part to-morrow night, let us remember that we owe it to our country and to mankind that this war shall have for its conclusion the establishing of the principle of democratic government—the simple principle that whatever party, whatever portion of the community, prevails by constitutional suffrage in an election, that party is to be respected and maintained in power until it shall give place, on another trial and another verdict, to a different portion of the people. If you do not do this, you are drifting at once and irresistibly to the very verge of universal, cheerless and hopeless anarchy. But with that principle this government of ours—the purest, the best, the wisest, and the happiest in the world—must be, and, so far as we are concerned, practically will be, immortal. (Cheers.) Fellow citizens, good-night."

The crowd followed the music to seek other notabilities, and had the satisfaction of hearing short speeches from Representatives McPherson and McKnight, Judge Shannon, Wayne MacVeagh and others. These addresses were not altogether perfunctory. A certain political tension existed throughout the entire war period, which rarely failed to color every word of a public speaker, and attune the ear of every public listener to subtle and oracular meanings. Even in this ceremonial gathering there was a keen watchfulness for any sign or omen which might disclose a drift in popular feeling, either on the local Pennsylvania quarrel between Cameron and Curtin, or the final success or failure of the Emancipation Proclamation; or whether the President would or would not secure for himself a renomination and reelection in the coming campaign of 1864.

There were still here and there ultra-radical newspapers that suspected and questioned Seward's hearty support of the emancipation policy. These made favorable note of his little address in which he predicted that the war would end in the removal of slavery, and that "when that cause is removed, simply by the operation of abolishing it, as the origin and agent of the treason that is without justification, and without parallel, we shall henceforth be united, be only one country, having only one hope, one ambition and one destiny."

Colonel John W. Forney, a veteran newspaper man and a hard drinker, having drunk heavily all day, was called out by a serenade that Hay and others arranged for his benefit. Forney rebuked his hearers for giving him more hearty cheers than they had given the President, but he probably had no doubt that he deserved all the cheers that he received.

The President himself was in no mood for merriment. He was painfully aware that on the next morning he must

make a speech from the same platform that was to be occupied by a scholarly and eloquent orator.   Doctor Everett
had come on several days before, and was a guest in the
Wills house.   He and Governor Curtin and other distinguished men were at the table that night, and others
dropped in after dinner.   Lincoln was in no mood to respond
to the serenade; he wanted to get to work on his speech.

Between nine and ten he went to his room, accompanied
only by his colored servant, William.   He laid out his
papers, ready to write, and then asked William to go down
and ask Judge Wills to come up to him.   He questioned
Judge Wills carefully as to the arrangements for the following day, including the part which the President was expected
to take.   He did not ask for paper; he had it with him,
as Judge Wills noticed, and as the quality of the paper
attests.

About ten o'clock Judge Wills went down-stairs, and for
an hour he heard nothing from the President.   However,
he did not go to bed, if for no other reason than that William had not left and the President was therefore still at
work.   About eleven o'clock William came down again and
said that the President would like to see Judge Wills.   The
Judge went to the President's room, and Mr. Lincoln said
he would like to confer with Mr. Seward.   Judge Wills told
him that Mr. Seward was at the Harper house next door,
and offered to go and bring him; but Lincoln said, "No, I'll
go and see him."   The two went together, and Mr. Lincoln
carried in his hand the sheets of paper on which he had
been writing.   Seward was still up and Wills left the President with him.   About half past eleven the President returned, the manuscript still in his hand, and Wills noticed
the paper and was sure that it was the same kind of paper
which he saw in the President's hand next day.   He said
afterward, "The next day I sat by him on the platform

when he delivered the address, which has become immortal, and he read it from the same paper on which I had seen him writing it the night before."

In the light of all that we now know, it is safe to assert that what Lincoln carried over to read to Seward was the first draft, the second and outside sheet of which was on paper precisely like that which Lincoln used in rewriting the address next morning. Virtually, he finished it that night, and waited for the morning when he might copy it with care, and make any final alterations that came to him before the delivery.

Gradually the town had subsided into an approach to silence. Sheer physical weariness laid its heavy hand on the noisy crowds that had come to attend the dedication. The President, too, was weary. About midnight he lay down to sleep, surrounded by the spirits of the mighty dead, and devoutly praying that these honored dead should not have died in vain.

CHAPTER IX

What Lincoln Intended to Say

After his election to the presidency, Lincoln spoke little in public, and what he said he wrote out carefully. He was a morbidly cautious man, and he was painfully aware that for every idle word the President of the United States must give account in a daily judgment of the country expressed through the newspapers. It would have been an incredible thing that he should have made no preparation for an address to be delivered on such an occasion as the Gettysburg dedication. He had little time, but he did prepare.

He intended to make his address "short, very short." He told Noah Brooks so, on Sunday at Gardner's gallery. He had Everett's proof with him, and while he must have been painfully impressed with his inability, or supposed inability, to do anything so fine in the way of oratory, he was not foolish enough to suppose that he would be forgiven if he did nothing or if he did it badly. Already, on Sunday, November eighth, his address was begun.

On Monday, November seventeenth, he told Honorable James Speed, later a member of his Cabinet, that he had found time "to write about half of it." James Speed so reported in an interview in the *Louisville Commercial*, in November, 1870, which was only seven years after the event, and before there had been much controversy about the matter.

Whether Lincoln had wholly completed his first draft

before he left Washington, we are not quite sure; if he had, he was not satisfied with the way it ended. This much, at the very least, he had written, all in ink, on a single sheet of "Executive Mansion" letter-paper:

"Four score and seven years ago our fathers brought forth, upon this continent, a new nation, conceived in liberty, and dedicated to the proposition that 'all men are created equal.'

"Now we are engaged in a great civil war, testing whether that nation, or any nation so conceived, and so dedicated, can long endure. We are met on a great battle field of that war. We have come to dedicate a portion of it, as a final resting place for those who died here, that the nation might live. This we may, in all propriety do. But, in a larger sense, we can not dedicate—we can not consecrate—we can not hallow, this ground—The brave men, living and dead, who struggled here, have hallowed it, far above our poor power to add or detract. The world will little note, nor long remember what we say here; while it can never forget what they *did* here. It is rather for us, the living to stand here"

There the page ended. There were nineteen lines, carefully written in ink, all at a sitting as nearly as we may judge, and completely filling the sheet. It would appear almost certain that there was a second sheet of paper like the first, continuing the sentence, though whether completing it, we may not be sure. Lincoln had trouble with his last sentence.

He certainly did not write the address nor any large part of it on the train. It is possible that he produced an envelope, or pad, or whatever sort of paper witnesses thought they remembered to have seen him use, and penciled some words upon that. But that is the most he could have done on the way.

At Judge Wills' house that evening he read over the first draft of his speech, and was not pleased with the way it ended. His second sheet, whatever he had on it, he presumably destroyed. Except for this first sheet, he employed the wide-lined paper which he habitually used for public documents, precisely similar to that which he employed for the writing of the Second Inaugural. He took a new sheet of paper, marked out with his pencil the three words "to stand here" with which the first page ended, and in pencil, not pen, wrote above these "we here be dedica" On the new sheet he continued:

"ted to the great task remaining before us—that, from these honored dead we take increased devotion to that cause for which they here, gave the last full measure of devotion—that we here highly resolve these dead shall not have died in vain; that the nation, shall have a new birth of freedom, and that government of the people by the people for the people, shall not perish from the earth."

He walked across to the Harper house and read this to Seward, and Seward can not have made any important suggestions, or if he did so, they do not seem to have been regarded by Lincoln as important.

He worked no more upon his manuscript that night. The address had assumed an approach to finality, and Lincoln went to bed Wednesday night in the Wills house, with his address practically finished. About nine o'clock the following morning, Lincoln rose from the breakfast table in the Wills house and went to his room. There, not very long afterward, John G. Nicolay found him rewriting his address. For this rewriting he used the same kind of paper which he had used for the penciled first draft of his second page.* From the new draft, written wholly in ink, and without erasure, on two pages of the wide-lined paper Lincoln delivered his address that day. This second draft is virtually a fair copy of the first draft. The following is what Lincoln intended to say at Gettysburg:

"Four score and seven years ago our fathers brought forth, upon this continent, a new nation, conceived in Liberty, and dedicated to the proposition that all men are created equal.

"Now we are engaged in a great civil war, testing whether that nation, or any nation, so conceived, and so dedicated, can long endure. We are met here on a great battle-field of that war. We have come to dedicate a portion of it as a final resting place for those who here gave their lives that that nation might live. It is altogether fitting and proper that we should do this.

"But in a larger sense we can not dedicate—we can not consecrate—we can not hallow this ground. The brave men, living and dead, who struggled here, have consecrated it far above our poor power to add or detract. The world will little note, nor long remember, what we say here, but

---

*The statement often made that Lincoln used "a sheet of rough paper" or of bluish paper, or of any kind of paper which he might casually have picked up on the train or at the Wills house, is a mistake. The second sheet of the first draft is on the same kind of paper which he used for the whole of the second draft and was accustomed to use in the White House for his carefully written documents. It was of large letter size, not note or legal cap, and the widely spaced lines permitted room for interlineation or erasure. There is every reason to suppose that Lincoln took a supply of this paper with him from the White House. While we do not know anything about the second sheet of the original first draft, I assume that there was such a sheet, and that it was written on the Executive Mansion stationery as was the first sheet. We do not know how much was written on that sheet, but it is not reasonable to think that Lincoln broke off with the words "to stand here." His closing words concerning government of the people must have been clearly in his mind and he may be believed to have committed them to paper. But the difficulty he faced in the construction of his last sentence is obvious. Our actual knowledge is only what the manuscripts disclose.

can never forget what they did here. It is for us, the living, rather to be dedicated here to the unfinished work which they have thus far, so nobly carried on. It is rather for us to be here dedicated to the great task remaining before us—that from these honored dead we take increased devotion to that cause for which they here gave the last full measure of devotion—that we here highly resolve that these dead shall not have died in vain; that this nation shall have a new birth of freedom; and that this government of the people, by the people, for the people, shall not perish from the earth."

CHAPTER X

The Dedication

The authorities in charge of the dedication service assumed a perilous risk of bad weather, when, in order to give Mr. Everett time for preparation of his oration, they postponed the date from October twenty-third to November nineteenth. But the weather was propitious. The night preceding the celebration was clear and warm, and the moon shone bright. Gettysburg's usual population of about 1,333 was multiplied manyfold. Never, except during the battle, had so many people gathered there. Estimates of the numbers present vary all the way from fifteen thousand to one hundred thousand. The former figure is probably more nearly correct than the latter, and is large enough to suggest a crowd of embarrassing proportions.

The official order of the procession included places in line for a number of men who were not present, and not all who were there cared to march. So many found more pleasure in standing along the way to see the procession march past that there was danger that there would be no procession. This is the order as it was given on the Official Announcement:

ORDER OF PROCESSION

FOR THE

CONSECRATION OF THE NATIONAL CEMETERY AT GETTYSBURG, PA.,

ON THE 19TH OF NOVEMBER, 1863.

Military, under command of Major General COUCH.

Major General MEADE and Staff, and the Officers and
Soldiers of the Army of the Potomac.

Officers of the Navy and Marine Corps of the United States.

Aids.   CHIEF MARSHAL.   Aids.

PRESIDENT OF THE UNITED STATES.

Members of the Cabinet.

Assistant Secretaries of the several Executive Departments.

General-in chief of the Army, and Staff.

Lieutenant General SCOTT and Rear-Admiral STEWART.

Judges of the United States Supreme Court.

HON. EDWARD EVERETT, Orator of the Day, and the
Chaplain.

Governors of the States, and their Staffs.

Commissioners of the States on the Inauguration of the
Cemetery.

Bearers with the Flags of the States.

VICE PRESIDENT OF THE UNITED STATES and Speaker of
the House of Representatives.

Members of the two houses of Congress.

Officers of the two houses of Congress.

Mayors of Cities.

Gettysburg Committee of Arrangements.

Officers and members of the United States Sanitary Commission.

Committees of different Religious Bodies.

United States Military Telegraphic Corps.

Officers and representatives of Adams Express Company.

Officers of different Telegraph Companies.

Hospital Corps of the Army.

Soldiers' Relief Associations.

Knights Templar.

Masonic Fraternity.

Independent Order of Odd Fellows.

Other Benevolent Associations.

Washington, _____, 186

Four score and seven years ago our fathers brought
forth, upon this continent, a new nation, conceived
in liberty, and dedicated to the proposition that
"all men are created equal"

Now we are engaged in a great civil war, testing
whether that nation, or any nation so conceived,
and so dedicated, can long endure. We are met
on a great battle field of that war. We have
come to dedicate a portion of it, as a final rest=
ing place for those who died here, that the nation
might live. This we may, in all propriety do. But, in a
larger sense, we can not dedicate— we can not
consecrate— we can not hallow, this ground—
The brave men, living and dead, who struggled
here, have hallowed it, far above our poor power
to add or detract. The world will little note, nor long
remember what we say here; while it can never
forget what they did here.
It is rather for us, the living, we here be dedicate
to stand here,

First page of the first draft of the Gettysburg Address written in Washington (In ink
except last few words)

ted to the great task remaining before us— that, from these honored dead we take increased devotion to that cause for which they here, gave the last full measure of devotion— that we here highly resolve these dead shall not have died in vain; that the nation, shall have a new birth of freedom, and that government of the people by the people for the people, shall not perish from the earth.

Second page of the first draft of the Gettysburg Address written in Gettysburg the night before the Address (In pencil)

Literary, Scientific and Industrial Associations.
The Press.
Officers and Members of Loyal Leagues.
Fire Companies.
Citizens of the State of Pennsylvania.
Citizens of other States.
Citizens of the District of Columbia.
Citizens of the several Territories.

The marching order and program of exercises were as follows:

PROGRAMME OF ARRANGEMENTS,

AND ORDER OF EXERCISES FOR THE CONSECRATION OF THE NATIONAL CEMETERY, AT GETTYSBURG, ON THE 19TH OF NOVEMBER, 1863.

The military will form in Gettysburg at nine o'clock, A. M., on Carlisle street, north of the square, its right resting on the square, opposite M'Clellan's hotel, under the direction of Major General Couch.

The State Marshals and Chief Marshal's aids will assemble in the public square at the same hour.

All civic bodies, except the citizens of States, will assemble, according to the foregoing printed programme, on York street, at the same hour.

The delegation of Pennsylvania citizens will form on Chambersburg street, its right resting on the square; and the other citizen delegations, in their order, will form on the same street, in rear of the Pennsylvania delegation.

The Marshals of the States are charged with the duty of forming their several delegations so that they will assume their appropriate positions when the main procession moves.

The head of the column will move at precisely ten o'clock, A. M.

The route will be up Baltimore street to the Emmitsburg road, thence to the junction of the Taneytown road, thence, by the latter road, to the Cemetery, where the military will form in line, as the General in command may order, for the purpose of saluting the President of the United States.

The military will then close up and occupy the space on the left of the stand.

The civic procession will advance and occupy the area in front of the stand, the military leaving sufficient space between them and the line of graves for the civic procession to pass.

The ladies will occupy the right of the stand, and it is desirable that they be upon the ground as early as ten o'clock, A. M.

The exercises will take place as soon as the military and civic bodies are in position, as follows:

Music, by Birgfield's Band.

Prayer, by Rev. T. H. Stockton, D. D.

Music, by the Marine Band.

Oration, by Hon. Edward Everett.

Music, Hymn composed by B. B. French, Esq.

Dedicatory Remarks, by the President of the United States.

Dirge, sung by Choir selected for the occasion.

Benediction, by Rev. H. L. Baugher, D. D.

After the benediction the procession will be dismissed, and the State Marshals and special aids to the Chief Marshal, will form on Baltimore street, and return to the court house in Gettysburg, where a meeting of the Marshals will be held.

An appropriate salute will be fired in Gettysburg on the

day of the celebration, under the direction of Major General Couch.

While the procession was not all that a procession might have been, there was a procession of a sort. The United States Marine Band, of Washington, the Second United States Artillery Band, of Baltimore, the Birgfield Band, of Philadelphia, and the band of the Fifth New York Heavy Artillery, were in line and furnished music, and certain military organizations took their assigned places in line; the Cemetery Commissions from the several states were in their places; and the President and the three members of his Cabinet present appeared on horseback. But the vast concourse of people either stood on the sidewalks or hastened to the cemetery to secure advantageous positions.

The procession was to have started at ten o'clock. At that hour, Mr. Lincoln, dressed in black, and wearing a tall hat and white gauntlets, emerged from the home of Mr. Wills and mounted a waiting horse. The crowd pressed in upon him and he was compelled to hold an informal reception on horseback. It was eleven o'clock before the procession got under way. The President's horse was too small, and the President did not appear to good advantage.

When the President reached the cemetery, there was another delay. Mr. Everett had not arrived. He did not arrive for half an hour. The exercises began at noon, an hour late.

Colonel Carr, who rode just behind the President, stated that when the procession started, the President sat erect on his horse and looked the part of Commander-in-Chief of the Army; but as the procession moved on, his body leaned forward, his arms hung limp, and his head was bent. He seemed absorbed in thought. The route was only three-quarters of a mile long, and the march was over in little more than a quarter of an hour. The tedium of the wait for Mr. Everett was partly relieved by the music of the band. Noon arrived, and with it Governor Everett; and the formal proceedings began.

Effort had been made to secure a poem, to be set to music for the occasion, the words to have been written by Lowell, Longfellow, Whittier, Bryant or George Boker. None of these gentlemen responded favorably when request was made of them. On November twelfth, a week before the dedication, Gettysburg was visited by Ward Hill Lamon, who was to serve as marshal, and Benjamin B. French, Officer in Charge of Buildings in Washington. Mr. Wills informed them of his disappointment, and Mr. French before he left town next morning handed Mr. Wills the manuscript of a hymn which he had written on this short notice. It was rather surprisingly good.

Among the distinguished persons on the platform at the dedication, according to the Philadelphia *Press,* were the following: Governor Curtin, of Pennsylvania; Governor Bradford, of Maryland; Governor Morton, of Indiana; Governor Seymour, of New York; Governor Parker, of New Jersey; Ex-Governor Tod, of Ohio; Governor Dennison, of Ohio; John Brough, Governor-elect of Ohio; Major-Generals Schenck, Stahl, Doubleday and Couch; Brigadier-General Gibbon and Provost-Marshal General Fry. The reporter must have also seen among the notable visitors Secretary Seward, Marshal Lamon, and others about equally distinguished.

The ceremonies were opened with prayer by Reverend Thomas H. Stockton, Chaplain of the House of Representatives. A correspondent of the Philadelphia *Press,* states that "the reverend gentleman concluded with the Lord's prayer, and during the delivery of these eloquent words there was scarcely a dry eye in all that vast assemblage."

Edward Everett was in his day America's foremost orator. He had been a noted Boston minister; had followed
his work in the pulpit with ten years as a professor of
Greek; had then been successively President of Harvard,
Governor of Massachusetts, United States Senator, Minister to England and Secretary of State. He was a cultured
scholar, and an orator whose productions, based on the best
Greek models, displayed American scholarship upon the
platform at its best. He had delivered memorable orations
at historic spots in New England, notable in connection with
semi-centennial celebrations of battles in the Revolutionary
War. His oration on Washington, a hundred times repeated in many parts of the country, had brought in the
money that helped to purchase and save Mount Vernon.
He had been candidate for Vice-President on one of the
tickets opposed to Lincoln, but was a hearty supporter of
Lincoln's administration. America had no orator in his
generation, and has produced none since, who could more
worthily have represented the nation in a classic oration on
such an occasion as that which he met at Gettysburg.

Very properly, Doctor Everett had insisted upon sufficient time in which to make careful preparation for his
address. Having written it in full, he committed it to memory, and doubtless rehearsed it. Leaving nothing to chance,
he spent three days at Gettysburg and thoroughly studied
the field. He had already made use of reports prepared for
him by General Meade and others, and his allusions were
remarkably correct; but a threefold comparison of his
proofs, his manuscript and the final printed form of the
address shows that Everett revised as carefully as Lincoln.
His topographical allusions, already excellent, were made
still more accurate.

He had intended to begin with the words of what is
now the second paragraph, "It was appointed by law in

Athens," but evidently the solemnity of the occasion impressed him deeply as the hour approached, and he prefaced a paragraph in which was an appeal for sympathy in the great task that had been assigned to him:

"Standing beneath this serene sky, overlooking these broad fields now reposing from the labors of the waning year, the mighty Alleghenies dimly towering before us, the graves of our brethren beneath our feet, it is with hesitation that I raise my poor voice to break the eloquent silence of God and Nature. But the duty to which you have called me must be performed;—grant me, I pray you, your indulgence and your sympathy."

That paragraph discloses the sincere humility of a truly noble mind. With whatever of reliance he may have placed on his oratorical power and his wealth of scholarship, he felt in the presence of the occasion that combination of quiet courage and of diffidence which are possible only to great spirits.

He spoke without reference to his manuscript or consultation of any notes. He had gone carefully over his address as written and had timed it and marked in the margin just what portions he would omit. His mind and utterance moved from paragraph to paragraph with sure tread. His sentences were perfectly balanced. Even his gestures appeared to have been, and probably had been, rehearsed and were faultless. It was oratory at its classic best.*

John Russell Young in his report said, "The populace gathered within a circle of great extent around the stand

---

*These comments are based on a study of Edward Everett's original manuscript of which the author owns a complete set of photostats, through the courtesy of Senator Keyes.

were so quiet and attentive that every word uttered by the
orator of the day (Edward Everett) must have been heard
by them all."

Mr. Everett spoke for an hour and fifty-seven minutes,
or as some hearers affirm, a trifle over two hours. From
the beginning to the end he held the attention of the
thoughtful among his hearers. His white hair, his erect
form, his graceful pose, his faultless gesticulation, his becoming attire, his poise, his self-control, his clear high
voice, his knowledge, precision and oratorical power, held
his audience remarkably; for his closing words were uttered
three hours after most of the people had taken their places
before the platform. The idle and the restless moved
away, but the more thoughtful ones in the assembly heard
him with interest unabated until the very end of his eloquent
peroration.

At the close of Everett's address, Mr. French's hymn
was sung, and under all the circumstances it was not unworthy of the occasion. Then Honorable Ward Hill Lamon introduced the President of the United States, who
rose and made a few appropriate remarks. And the world
has long remembered what he said there.

CHAPTER XI

What He Said and How He Said It

If Lincoln had read his address literally from his manuscript, the second draft would tell us what he said. But he did not. We have our usual conflict of testimony between those who thought he read it entire and those who thought he did not read it at all; but we are sure that he recited the greater part of it from memory.

He was nervous as the time approached for him to speak. He knew the content of Everett's oration, and was aware when his own time was approaching. He drew out his manuscript, adjusted his spectacles, shifted his position in his chair, and reviewed his speech. Virtually he had learned it by heart. He could have delivered it without any manuscript. Standing firmly on both feet, he held his manuscript in both hands, and glanced at it infrequently.

Mr. Lincoln commenced his speech in his high, thin and rather metallic, but clear voice. He always began in that way when he spoke out-of-doors. It took him all of ten minutes to get down to his own natural tone, and that was high for a man of his stature. When people heard him and Douglas on the same platform they almost invariably remarked that the little man had the big voice and the big man the little voice. Lincoln's voice was not falsetto and not effeminate, but it was of high pitch habitually, and was particularly so when he felt under constraint to make a large company hear. His voice carried well, and he did not wear it out. Douglas, with a deep rich baritone, had a long uvula, and that irritated his throat. He abused his voice, and often was not well heard, but Lincoln made his audiences hear. They heard at Gettysburg. All who were in position near the platform heard; if any did not, it was those who had strayed during the latter part of Everett's long oration.

Do we know what Lincoln actually said?

We do, or at least we may. We can not learn his actual words from his written manuscript, nor yet from the Associated Press report, for its stenography was incomplete, and the words were partially written in afterward from Lincoln's manuscript. Fortunately, the manuscript did not supply the whole of that report. But Massachusetts, a state deeply interested in this event, and with a Governor, John A. Andrew, vitally concerned in the success of the war, had a strong official representation at Gettysburg. One of its three men was Charles Hale, of the Boston *Advertiser*, a brother of Edward Everett Hale. He had notebook and pencil in hand, and as Lincoln spoke very slowly, Mr. Hale was positive that he caught every word. He took down what he declared was the exact language of Lincoln's address, and his declaration is as good as the oath of a court stenographer. His associates confirmed his testimony, which was received, as it deserved to be, at its face value, by Governor Andrew. Here is what Lincoln actually said at Gettysburg:

"Fourscore and seven years ago, our fathers brought forth upon this continent a new nation, conceived in liberty and dedicated to the proposition that all men are created equal.

"Now we are engaged in a great civil war, testing whether that nation—or any nation, so conceived and so dedicated—can long endure.

"We are met on a great battle-field of that war. We are met to dedicate a portion of it as the final resting-place of those who have given their lives that that nation might live.

"It is altogether fitting and proper that we should do this.

"But, in a larger sense, we cannot dedicate, we cannot consecrate, we cannot hallow, this ground. The brave men, living and dead, who struggled here, have consecrated it, far above our power to add or to detract.

"The world will very little note nor long remember what we say here; but it can never forget what they did here.

"It is for us, the living, rather, *to be dedicated,* here, to the unfinished work that they have thus far so nobly carried on. It is rather for us to be here dedicated to the great task remaining before us; that from these honored dead we take increased devotion to that cause for which they here gave the last full measure of devotion; that we here highly resolve that these dead shall not have died in vain; that the nation shall, under God, have a new birth of freedom, and that government of the people, by the people, for the people, shall not perish from the earth."

While most of the newspapers depended upon the Associated Press reports, the Cincinnati *Commercial* was one of the papers that had a report of its own. The reporter, wiring his comment that afternoon, gave this concise and convincing description:

"The President rises slowly, draws from his pocket a paper, and, when commotion subsides, in a sharp, unmusical treble voice, reads the following brief and pithy remarks."

In all the five versions of the address written by Lincoln he spoke of "our poor power." In the second copy he first omitted the adjective, and then wrote it in above. Gilbert, in his version for the Associated Press, used the adjective, but he had Lincoln's manuscript and copied from that. Neither of the other accounts used the word "poor." It is evident, therefore, that in the delivery, Lincoln omitted it, doubtless inadvertently. But when he came to revise his speech, though he must have been reminded that he had not actually used the word, he wrote it definitely into the address as he wished it to be remembered.

An interesting question arises, and I have asked it of a number of men who heard the address: "What words did Lincoln emphasize in his last sentence? Did he say 'government *of* the people, *by* the people, *for* the people,' or did he say 'government of the *people,* by the *people,* for the *people'?"*

In general the men to whom I have propounded this question did not claim to remember, and most of them had not thought about it. They thought he emphasized the prepositions, but they were not sure. Indeed, they were so vague in their recollections that I do not regard their testimony on this point as of any value, and each reader may do his own guessing as to the emphasis which Lincoln would have been likely to give. I should rather like to think that he gave the preposition its full value, but imparted his emphasis to the word "people."

Colonel Clark E. Carr, who added to his other qualifications for discourse on this subject, a gift of mimicry, would sometimes entertain his friends by reciting passages from Lincoln and from Douglas as he remembered to have heard them. And of course he recited the Gettysburg Address. He emphasized about equally as I heard him, the prepositions and the words "the people."

CHAPTER XII

What He Was Reported to Have Said

Considering how small a town Gettysburg was, and how meager its telegraphic facilities must have been, the Gettysburg dedication was well reported. The program and the full text of Mr. Everett's address had been mailed out to newspapers in all parts of the country in adequate time for both to be set up and ready for the press. A "release" paragraph, about a "stick" in length, was wired from Gettysburg early in the day, saying that the weather was fine and that the program was carried out as printed. Such local color as was needed in advance was supplied by accounts of the evening before; indeed, in one or more papers "the President's Address" was his little talk of the preceding evening refusing to make an address! But this was exceptional. Most of the large papers contained his speech, delivered about half past two, in ample time for their morning issues.

But the report of the dedication itself was crowded by the space already assigned to Everett, and by other important happenings. The ship *Peru* had just arrived in New York, bringing a report of the convening of the French Assembly, and the speech of Emperor Napoleon III. That had to be printed. Henry Ward Beecher was just back from England, after a tempestuous experience, and on the night when Lincoln was refusing to talk in response to the serenade, Beecher was doing the very reverse in New York. Three front-page columns of the New York

84

Times were assigned to Beecher, and two to the Gettysburg celebration, under the caption "Honor Heroes of July." Another column had to go to Burnside, who had done a not very important thing in Knoxville. Johnnie Heenan was arranging for a fight to a decision for the champion belt and a purse of two thousand pounds, his contestant being an Englishman named King, and patriotism demanded that King should be knocked out. An army officer had lodgings in the house of a widow, whose name can be found by those interested in the matter, and the said widow went into court, claiming that he had called upon her for privileges over and above his room and board, and she demanded pay for all, including a broken heart; and the evidence in this case had to be published for the enlightenment of the public.

It was rather fortunate for Abraham Lincoln that, coming at the end of the program, and with such competition for attention in the newspaper columns, he got any space for his address; but there were only two sticksful of it, and room was made for him.

It is not possible to be sure just how many shorthand reports there were. Counting that of Charles Hale as the most reliable, and that of Joseph L. Gilbert of the Associated Press, which was made up hastily, partly from his own notes and partly from Lincoln's manuscript, there was at least one other report, and it is probable there were two. The Associated Press report was used by the New York *Tribune* and the *Herald,* the Boston *Advertiser* and the *Journal,* the Springfield *Republican,* the *Ledger* and *North American* of Philadelphia, the *Commercial* of Cincinnati, and by many newspapers in other cities. Such variations as occur are evidently due to mistakes in telegraphing or transcribing. The Philadelphia *Inquirer* and the Cincinnati *Gazette* printed reports that are in some respects alike but differ sufficiently to make it probable that they were made by two different reporters, neither of them very accurate.*

The Associated Press report as contained in the New York *Tribune* is as follows:

"Four score and seven years ago our fathers brought forth upon this continent a new Nation, conceived in Liberty, and dedicated to the proposition that all men are created equal. [Applause.] Now we are engaged in a great civil war, testing whether that Nation or any Nation so conceived and so dedicated can long endure. We are met on a great battle-field of that war. We are met to dedicate a portion of it as the final resting-place of those who here gave their lives that that nation might live. It is altogether fitting and proper that we should do this. But in a larger sense we cannot dedicate, we cannot consecrate, we cannot hallow this ground. The brave men living and dead who struggled here have consecrated it far above our power to add or detract. [Applause.] The world will little note nor long remember what we say here, but it can never forget what they did here. [Applause.] It is for us, the living, rather to be dedicated here to the unfinished work that they have thus far so nobly carried on. [Applause.] It is rather for us to be here dedicated to the great task remaining before us, that from these honored dead we take increased devotion to that cause for which they here gave the last full measure of devotion; that we here highly resolve that the dead shall not have died in vain [Applause.]; that the nation shall, under God, have a new birth of freedom; and that governments of the people, by the people and for the people, shall not perish from the earth. [Long-continued applause.]"

---

*While the New York *Tribune* had its own reporter at Gettysburg, and that paper's report of the address differs slightly from the Associated Press report as it appeared in other papers, I am confident that it was based on the same script.

The Philadelphia *Inquirer* had its own version, which was the one used in the local report in the Gettysburg *Compiler*:

"Four score and seven years ago our fathers brought forth upon this continent a new nation, conceived in liberty and dedicated to the proposition that all men are created equal. Now we are engaged in a great civil war, testing the question whether this nation or any nation so conceived, so dedicated, can long endure. We are met on the great battlefield of that war. We are met to dedicate it, on a portion of the field set apart as the final resting place of those who gave their lives for the nation's life; but the nation must live, and it is altogether fitting and proper that we should do this.

"In a larger sense we cannot dedicate, we cannot consecrate, we cannot hallow this ground in reality. The number of men, living and dead, who struggled here have consecrated it far above our poor attempts to add to its consecration. The world will little know and nothing remember of what we see here, but we cannot forget what these brave men did here.

"We owe this offering to our dead. We imbibe increased devotion to that cause for which they here gave the last full measure of devotion; we here might resolve that they shall not have died in vain; that the nation shall, under God, have a new birth of freedom, and that the Government of the people, for the people, and for all people, shall not perish from earth."

All in all, we may conclude that the variations in these reports were less than might have been expected, especially in the light of the very great freedom with which the earlier biographers of Lincoln handled the text.

During the administration of President Coolidge, an organization that had secured an appointment at the White House determined to leave for the President of the United States, as a token of their esteem, a tablet with the Gettysburg Address engraved upon it. The text of the address as published in the papers at the time, showed only twenty-eight errors!

But it is not only in the Gettysburg Address that Lincoln is misquoted. His words in that document are more nearly correctly broadcast than those taken from any other of his utterances. Much that is attributed to Lincoln would have surprised him.

CHAPTER XIII

How the Address Was Received

In her little work of fiction, *The Perfect Tribute,* which has become for many readers the authentic story of the Gettysburg Address, Mrs. Andrews relates that Lincoln was depressed by the failure of the crowd to applaud his address, but was much comforted when a wounded Confederate soldier told him that the reason there was no applause was that the people were so deeply moved by the nobility of the President's words that they would have counted applause a form of profanation. As far as is known, no such incident occurred. When we come to read the reports of eye-witnesses we shall find every variety of recollection as to the effect of the address upon those who heard it. Such opinion as we form must be the result of a judicial process, and not of any possible harmonization of the evidence. Yet the essential facts are reasonably clear.

There was applause when he rose. Everett had been applauded as he closed, and nothing less than applause would have been a decent greeting to the President. How hearty or general that applause was, we need not consider.

There may have been a little scattering applause as he proceeded, though that is not certain. The notes of the Associated Press reporter do not pretend to accuracy in this regard. The applause was of such a character that men like Colonel Carr could not feel sure that it had occurred. There must have been some applause at the end, but it certainly was not enthusiastic. Mr. French, already

89

in the seventh heaven over the singing of his hymn, and almost intoxicated with the glory that had descended upon him in having been permitted to sit on the platform near the President when that hymn was sung, wrote on the next Sunday morning:

"Abraham Lincoln is the idol of the American people at this moment. Any one who saw and heard the hurricane of applause that met his every word at Gettysburg, would know that he lived in every heart."

That, however, was not a sober judgment. There was applause, but no hurricane. John Hay was favorably impressed, but not enthusiastic. He said that the President "in a firm, free way, with more grace than is his wont, said his half-dozen lines of consecration. And the music wailed and we went home through crowded and cheering streets."

In the narratives of both French and Hay it was the President rather than his speech that was applauded.

I once inquired of Robert T. Lincoln if he thought his father was satisfied with the effects of the address, and he said that he was not in the White House at the time, and had no recollection of hearing his father speak of it, but in view of Everett's compliment, alleged to have been paid to Lincoln before he left the platform, and repeated in a letter the next day, he thought his father probably felt that he had done well. However, Robert Lincoln did not pretend to know.

Mr. Everett knew how to pay a graceful compliment, and he did pay it. But nothing in his letter proves that he thought Lincoln had reached the audience before him.

Lincoln did not think he had succeeded. As wet soil sticks to the mold-board of a rusty plow, so he felt that his speech "did not scour."

John Russell Young was present as a special representative of the Philadelphia *Press*. He sat on the platform, and apparently did not himself make a stenographic report of the address, but depended for that on the Associated Press report. In 1891 he published an article in which he gave his own recollections, based on his notes made at the time, and he said:

"The report of the Associated Press was studded with applause, and I do not remember the applause, and am afraid the appreciative reporter was more than generous— may have put in the applause as a personal expression of opinion. . . . I have read of the emotions produced by the President's address, the transcendent awe that fell upon every one who heard those most mighty and ever living words, to be remembered with pride through the ages. I have read of the tears that fell and the solemn hush, as though in a cathedral solemnity in the most holy moment of the Sacrifice. There was nothing of this, to the writer at least, in the Gettysburg Address."

What impression did the people receive who actually heard Abraham Lincoln at Gettysburg? The correct answer is, no doubt, that there were as many different impressions as there were kinds of people in the audience. Yet if we may undertake a mental compositive photograph of that crowd, we may generalize with reasonable accuracy.

First, the people, having become somewhat weary during the long address of Everett, began to draw closer and to assume a new attitude of attention as the President rose, and their first concern was conditioned by the positions which they secured. Whether they were near the platform or farther back, they found themselves able to hear. But his seemed a thin high voice for so tall a man.

The next thing that impressed the people was Lincoln's

intonation. They had not thought of him as a native of Kentucky, but his pronunciation showed his origin. Speaking very slowly, as he had exhorted his neighbor, James C. Conkling, to do in reading his letter in Springfield, he tended to exaggerate, if anything, his native intonation. He pronounced the preposition "to" as if it were written "toe." He passed lightly over the sound of the letter "r." When he spoke of "our poor power," he showed his Kentucky idiom in every word. The prairies had done something for him, but most of his Illinois neighbors were of Kentucky stock. The President talked as they talked.

The next thing that the people noticed was that Lincoln stopped just as they thought he was beginning. Speaking very slowly, he was on his feet less than three minutes. He had not yet come to a common understanding with his audience. After Everett's oration the President's speech seemed almost no speech at all. People were disappointed.

The crowds began departing from Gettysburg four hours before the President's special train withdrew. People who had come by rail returned by regular or special trains to Philadelphia, Harrisburg, Baltimore and intermediate points, and were home by bedtime. Those who had traveled from the farms or villages near by, made their way homeward over roads that were solid and firm, not yet cut by late fall rains or frozen into winter ruts. The people were too weary to talk much that night about what they had seen and heard, but they told their neighbors about the celebration, the bands, the procession and the other outstanding incidents of the day. They told of hearing Everett and of seeing the President. Incidentally, some of them mentioned that the President had uttered a few remarks; yes, they had heard the President. But while they were glad to have heard him, not many of them at the time said very much about the President's speech.

CHAPTER XIV

THE SAME AFTERNOON

BECAUSE of the lateness of Mr. Everett's arrival at the cemetery, and the length of his address, it was after half past two when the dedication service ended. It was after three when the President got back to his room at the Wills house. The lunch had long been waiting.

President Lincoln, Governor Andrew G. Curtin, Honorable Edward Everett and other distinguished guests partook of luncheon at the Wills home. As that function had been cut short at one end by the eloquence of Doctor Everett, so was it cut at the other end by the desire of the public to see and shake hands with President Lincoln.

It was remarked then by Professor Calvin Hamilton that the President appeared sad and listless, and that his thoughts seemed to be far away while he was mechanically taking the hands of those who passed in procession. But he stopped a very tall man, and held his hand and spoke to him for a moment some word which Hamilton did not hear. This was thoroughly characteristic of Lincoln. Repeatedly at public receptions he stood absent-mindedly shaking hands and thinking of other matters, but he would come to life if a little boy or girl passed in line, and if a very tall man approached, Lincoln almost invariably stopped him and asked how tall he was.

This reception lasted from four o'clock till nearly five. Then the President passed out through Mr. Wills' office and went to the Presbyterian Church, where a patriotic meeting had been announced for five o'clock.

In that meeting the President divided honors with a local hero, John Burns. He was the village cobbler, and had been constable. It was his duty to preserve peace and good order in Gettysburg, and when the fight began on July first he did his best. Learning that the Confederates were approaching town by way of the Chambersburg road, he took down his powder-horn, filled his pockets with home-run bullets, shouldered his flint-lock squirrel rifle, and started out to put down the rebellion.

He fell in with the One Hundred and Fiftieth Pennsylvania Volunteers, who smiled at the seventy-year-old squirrel hunter, but let him remain with them. For a time they held the McPherson barn and the adjacent woods and then fell back. He did not retreat with them, but found the Iron Brigade, and fought with them. They, too, were forced back, but he stood beside a tree that is still pointed out, and continued firing till he was wounded three times and captured by the Confederates.

They did not take him far, nor did his wounds keep him away from the dedication service. When Lincoln heard about him, he asked to meet John Burns. The tall President and the short little constable walked side by side through Gettysburg streets.

Few are the people in Gettysburg who remember that scene, but those who witnessed it were accustomed to describe vividly the march of the long-legged President, and the toddling gait of the little old constable as he tried to keep alongside. Baltimore Street has not beheld a more interesting event to this day. Together the tall President and the squat constable walked down the aisle of the Presbyterian Church that had served as a hospital during the battle. In that church is still proudly shown the pew where Abraham Lincoln and John Burns sat for an hour side by side.

Mr. Wills was an elder in the Presbyterian Church, and it was he who planned that afternoon service and arranged for the attendance of the President. Colonel Anderson, Lieutenant-Governor-elect from Ohio, was the orator. Lincoln could not remain to the end. The special train was due to leave at six-thirty, and the President had to depart before the service concluded.

Edward Everett and his friends accompanied the President and his party on the special train back to Washington. But every one was weary, and most of those on the train were in no mood for conversation. Enough had been said for one day.

Lincoln had his manuscript in his pocket. He had lent it for a few moments to Joseph L. Gilbert, reporter for the Associated Press. Gilbert had started to take down the address, but seeing that Lincoln had the manuscript, he stopped, or at least made only incomplete notes. He made some attempt to correct his notes from the President's own manuscript, but did not have time for an accurate comparison. He completed his own report and sent it out by wire. We may well be grateful that he did not have more time. And we are grateful also that other reports made that day confirm his shorthand notes in one very important particular, even as Lincoln himself adjudged it.

On the journey to Washington, Lincoln talked but little. He lay down on one of the side-seats in the "drawing-room" and had a wet towel laid across his eyes and forehead. It was after midnight when the special train reached Washington, and Lincoln was more than ready for bed.

After the assassination of President Lincoln, a memorial service was held in the Presbyterian Church at Gettysburg. This was not done on the Sunday immediately following, as in many churches was the case, but on June first, the day which President Andrew Johnson proclaimed as one of na-

tional mourning. The pastor, the Reverend D. T. Carnahan, had half of April and all of May in which to prepare
his discourse. The sermon was printed. We might expect
to find it interspersed with such expressions as:

"Who of us here present can fail to remember with
thrilling pride the day when Abraham Lincoln trod these
streets, walked down the aisle of this very church, joined
with us in this holy place in the worship of God, and within
this town uttered his immortal address?"

One reads through that orthodox, loyal and dignified
production, and finds in it no indication that Mr. Carnahan
supposed that Lincoln had done anything noteworthy in that
town. Speaking to people, practically every one of whom
had heard the President speak, he stirred no deep memory
within them. He did not know and they did not know that
the event which he did not think important enough to
mention was that which was to make Gettysburg immortal.

CHAPTER XV

What He Wished He Had Said

LINCOLN returned from Gettysburg to Washington a sick man. At first he thought fatigue was all that ailed him, but it was more than that. He was eager to continue work on his message to Congress, which body was to convene in less than three weeks, and there was much routine business besides. In addition to all this, he had set his heart upon his Amnesty Proclamation, which might be said to be for Confederate soldiers living, what his Gettysburg Address was for the Union soldiers dead—a tribute and a declaration of confidence. This Amnesty Proclamation was one of his dearest achievements. He had enough on his hands for a man in robust health.

On Thursday, November twenty-sixth, John Hay recorded in his diary: "The President is sick in bed. Billious."

He did not officially change that diagnosis. But he wrote to Nicolay, who was just then out of the city, entreating him not to send to him (Hay) any more people who wanted him to ask favors of Stanton; Hay said he would rather run the risk of a smallpox ward in a hospital! That was, indeed, precisely what he was doing, and the President was the principal attraction in that ward. Gideon Welles recorded in his diary:

"I was invited and strongly urged by the President to attend the ceremonials at Gettysburg, but was compelled to decline, for I could not spare the time. The President re-

97

turned ill, and in a few days it was ascertained that he had
the varioloid. We were in Cabinet meeting when he informed us that the physician had on the preceding evening
ascertained and pronounced the nature of the complaint. It
was in light form, but yet held on stronger than was
expected. He would have avoided an interview, but wished
to submit and have our views of the message. All were
satisfied, and that portion which is his own displays sagacity
and wisdom."

Sick as Lincoln was on the morning after his return
from Gettysburg, he got out of bed to see "an intelligent
woman in deep distress" whose husband was sentenced to be
shot on the following Monday. The President promised
to do what he could for her and at once wired General
Meade to suspend the execution. Lincoln was troubled,
however, by the fact that the information which he found
in his hand after the woman had left was indefinite. She
had signed her own name "Mrs. Anna S. King," and said
her husband was a lieutenant, but Lincoln did not find her
husband's name or the number of the regiment in the
memoranda which she left. He kept thinking about this
woman and her husband, and later in the day he got up
again and sent General Meade a longer telegram to make
sure that the man should not be shot.

Mrs. Lincoln was sent out of the White House when
the nature of her husband's sickness was known. Once a
day or oftener Lincoln telegraphed her of his progress.
His usual form of telegram was: "Mrs. A. Lincoln, New
York. All going well. A. Lincoln."

Mrs. Lincoln returned to the White House during the
second week in December. At the time of her return, the
White House had a visitor whose coming brought some
aspects of the war very near to the hearts of President and

Mrs. Lincoln. Mrs. Emily Todd Helm, Mrs. Lincoln's youngest half-sister, came through the Confederate lines and to the White House under a flag of truce. She was a soul in bereavement. Her husband, General Ben Hardin Helm, had been killed. The Lincoln family was in a strait betwixt two deep emotions—sympathy for the bereaved "little sister" and stern loyalty to duty, together with no little concern regarding the spying and misrepresentation that were then in full vogue concerning Mrs. Lincoln's own loyalty to her country. On Monday, December fourteenth, Senator Browning, of Illinois, wrote in his diary:

"The President told me his sister-in-law, Mrs. Helm, was in the White House, but he did not wish it known. She wished an order for the protection of some cotton she had at Jackson, Mississippi. He thought she ought to have it, but he was afraid that he would be censured if he did so."

However, she got the order and was sent back to her home in Kentucky with a pass from President Lincoln. Fortunately the critics did not know much about it at the time, or Lincoln's anticipation of criticism would have been fully realized. I do not know what Lincoln himself would have said if he had known how much quinine for Southern hospitals she took back sewed in her petticoats.

Christmas was coming, and not a very cheerful Christmas at the White House, but Lincoln tried to make it a happy one for others. He signed some pardons in order that prisoners might celebrate Christmas at home. His old friend and political opponent, Honorable U. F. Linder, of Chicago, had a son Dan whose pronounced copperhead principles took him into the Confederate Army, though he was a resident of Illinois. He was captured, and the case against him was a serious one, but a day or two before

Christmas, Lincoln wired to the officer who had him in charge to bring young Linder to Washington, and he wired the father that he was sending Dan home as a Christmas present.

From the time of Lincoln's submitting his Amnesty Proclamation he labored with a special zeal to avoid punishment wherever possible. In commuting the sentence of one man who had been ordered shot he said: "The case is really a very bad one as appears by the record already before me." Yet Lincoln changed the sentence to imprisonment "not on any merit in the case but because I am trying to evade a butchering business lately." When General Banks wrote him concerning some people whom he had encountered who refused to take the Amnesty oath, declaring that they had never been disloyal, Lincoln replied expressing the wish that even so, if they had been accused of disloyalty, they would take the oath; but he said that if General Banks saw fit to deal with these people in any milder method, he was at liberty to do so.

These were some of the many concerns that occupied the mind of Abraham Lincoln in the days of the revision of the Gettysburg Address.

Sick, and that with smallpox, Lincoln convened his Cabinet. To that body he submitted his message and his Amnesty Proclamation, and both documents won the unanimous approval of his official advisers. He had come a far cry since December, 1862, when his Cabinet was so divided and discredited that the Senate was demanding a new one. John Hay was right. The Tycoon was in fine whack, and was running the government and managing the war.

His sickness did not keep the office-seekers away. "Come in," called Lincoln cheerfully from his bed. "I have something now that I can give to everybody!"

He was very happy about his Amnesty Proclamation.

It was issued on December 8, 1863, the day that the Congress convened. It was Lincoln's first day back at his desk. He was apologizing to Governor Curtin and others for delayed correspondence "on account of my sickness, and the preparation of my Message to Congress." But he was feeling very cheerful. This Amnesty Proclamation was to enable, and did enable, many thousands of former Confederates to take the oath of allegiance and be released from prison. There is a further story about that, also. Several hundred former Confederates who professed to desire to take the oath were refused, because of their previous bad record, or by reason of suspicion that they intended to take the oath "from the teeth out." It was no part of Lincoln's duty as President to review those cases, but toward the end of the war he made it his business. He was so eager to get every possible Confederate out of jail and back on his farm, that his last days, crowded as they were to the very limit, were occupied, whenever he had a spare moment, in looking over these papers and ordering the release of prisoners. I own several of these documents. On April 12, 1865, he was working alone, and he wrote with his own hand:

"Let this man be released on taking the oath of Dec. 8, 1863.

"A. Lincoln
"April 12, 1865."

But, hindered in this labor of love by multifarious interruptions, and perhaps with some prophetic premonition that he must make haste, on the following day he called for John Hay's assistance, and as he approved the few that he had time to read, he passed them over to his secretary, who wrote the endorsement, and Lincoln signed it:

"Let the Prisoner be released on taking the oath of
Dec. 8, 1863.

"A. Lincoln.
"April 13, 1865."

Crowded as was his next and last day, he found time to
sign a few of these papers just before the assassin's bullet
stopped his pen.

Fighting sickness after his return from Gettysburg, and
toiling from then to the end with a wan and happy smile
through the heavy tasks of his last months down to his last
conscious hours, Abraham Lincoln was thinking how he
could employ his energies to their utmost in the interests of
those men whom he had been fighting, but fighting without
hate. His life till its end was filled with deeds of mercy.

These details would have no rightful place in the present narrative except that they are a part of the Gettysburg
story. While Lincoln was preparing his Amnesty Proclamation, he was also revising his Gettysburg Address, and
offering to dispense smallpox freely among the office-seekers. It is all one story.

A speaker's inspirations do not cease with the platform.
When the tumult and the shouting have died, and the speaker is alone in his bed, weary and perhaps ashamed of himself, he is very likely to rehearse his speech and think of
the things he ought to have said. That is what drives
orators wild. If they could only have been as eloquent on
the platform as they are in bed the following night! Why
were they such fools as to say this? Why such idiots as not
to have thought of that? And so the clock strikes again
and again while the orator wearily rehearses the speech he
wishes he had made.

Let us hope that Abraham Lincoln was weary enough
when he reached Washington at midnight to go to sleep.

Four days later he was asked for the original manuscript of his address, and he did not give it. Mr. Wills wrote to him, on behalf of the Governors of the several states, asking him to send "the original manuscript" of his "dedicatory remarks . . . to be placed with the correspondence and other papers connected with the project."

The President examined the original draft, and it did not altogether please him. "By his direction, therefore, his secretaries made copies of the Associated Press reports as it was printed in several prominent newspapers. Comparing these with his own original draft, and with his own fresh recollection of the form in which he delivered it, he made a new autograph copy." So wrote John G. Nicolay.

We do not know what became of that new autograph copy. Perhaps Lincoln made it on the margin of a press report pasted on paper, and had it copied in another hand by one of his secretaries. Mr. Wills should be our best authority on this subject, but his testimony is not quite clear. In an early account he is alleged to have said that he did not remember in what form he received President Lincoln's address but that it was not an autograph copy. He told Major William H. Lambert that the copy received was not in Lincoln's handwriting. In another statement, made many years later, he said:

"He [Lincoln] afterward made a copy of it of which I have a facsimile, and have had a photograph of it taken."

I judge that Mr. Wills never owned an autograph copy of the address, but that, years afterward, coming upon a facsimile of one of the autograph forms, he thought it to have been like one that he had owned. Certainly no autograph copy, or facsimile of an autograph copy of the address in the form of this, its first revision subsequent to its delivery, is known to exist. Probably Lincoln made corrections on the margin of one of the proofs or copies made by his secretaries, and, being sick, left them to copy it and send to Mr. Wills. The changes that Lincoln made for Judge Wills to use in the official Gettysburg volume are rather curious, and several of them Lincoln later changed back again.

This is the first revision after delivery, and was made for and used in the official Gettysburg volume published by the state of Pennsylvania in 1863:

"DEDICATORY ADDRESS
OF
PRESIDENT LINCOLN

"Fourscore and seven years ago our fathers brought forth upon this continent a new nation, conceived in Liberty, and dedicated to the proposition that all men are created equal.

"Now we are engaged in a great civil war, testing whether that nation, or any nation so conceived and so dedicated, can long endure. We are met on a great battle-field of that war. We are met to dedicate a portion of it as the final resting-place of those who here gave their lives that that nation might live. It is altogether fitting and proper that we should do this.

"But in a larger sense we cannot dedicate, we cannot consecrate, we cannot hallow this ground. The brave men, living and dead, who struggled here have consecrated it far above our power to add or detract. The world will little note nor long remember what we say here, but it can never forget what they did here. It is for us, the living, rather to be dedicated here to the unfinished work that they have thus far so nobly carried on. It is rather for us to be here dedicated to the great task remaining before us—that from

these honored dead we take increased devotion to the cause
for which they here gave the last full measure of devotion—that we here highly resolve that the dead shall not
have died in vain; that the nation shall, under God, have a
new birth of freedom, and that the government of the
people, by the people, and for the people, shall not perish
from the earth."

And now a notable change came over the mind of Lincoln. As he grew better of his smallpox, he began to think
better of his Gettysburg Address. The compliment which
he received from Everett pleased him greatly. He showed
it to his friends. Everett said, "I should be glad if I could
flatter myself that I came as near to the central idea of the
occasion in two hours as you did in two minutes." Honorable James Speed, Lincoln's old friend and later his Attorney-General, said:

"He told me that he had never received a compliment
he prized more highly than that contained in a letter from
Edward Everett, written to him a few days after that
speech was delivered, and commenting upon it. He produced the letter, and allowed me to read it. It was as complimentary as it possibly could have been. I do not
remember its expression, but I remember well the extremely
handsome and flattering tone of the letter."

Everett did more. He wrote to Lincoln saying that
there was to be a great Sanitary Fair in New York, and
that the ladies who had it in charge had asked him for the
manuscript of his address. Everett had promised to give
them his manuscript and he requested the President to give
his manuscript also, that the two might be bound up in one
volume and sold for the benefit of sick soldiers.

By this time Lincoln had begun to think that his Gettysburg speech was not altogether a failure. If a manuscript copy of it was to be bound up with the speech of Everett, he wanted it to be in better form than any he had written up to that time. He took the matter in hand and gave the address a good overhauling.

The manuscript volume, now owned by Senator Keyes, of New Hampshire, shows some interesting facts. Everett worked his own address over, prefacing a paragraph to the printed form which he had sent out before delivery, and he caused a printed version to be bound in, face to face with the pages of his manuscript and that without proof-corrections in his own script. But when he came to examine Lincoln's new draft, he was struck by the changes Lincoln had made, and with his pen Everett made no less than ten proof corrections in the official form of Lincoln's address as it had been furnished by the President for the Pennsylvania volume, to make it conform to the new script which Lincoln sent to Everett. Though Lincoln was twice more to make copies of the address, the changes after the copy he made for Everett are unimportant. This is the form in which he sent the address to Edward Everett:

"Four score and seven years ago our fathers brought forth upon this continent, a new nation, conceived in Liberty, and dedicated to the proposition that all men are created equal.

"Now we are engaged in a great civil war, testing whether that nation, or any nation so conceived, and so dedicated, can long endure. We are met on a great battle-field of that war. We have come to dedicate a portion of that field, as a final resting place for those who here gave their lives, that that nation might live. It is altogether fitting and proper that we should do this.

"But, in a larger sense, we can not dedicate—we can not consecrate—we can not hallow—this ground. The brave men, living and dead, who struggled here, have consecrated it, far above our poor power to add or detract. The world will little note, nor long remember, what we say here, but it can never forget what they did here. It is for us, the living, rather, to be dedicated here to the unfinished work which they who fought here, have, thus far, so nobly advanced. It is rather for us to be here dedicated to the great task remaining before us—that from these honored dead we take increased devotion to that cause for which they here gave the last full measure of devotion—that we here highly resolve that these dead shall not have died in vain—that this nation, under God, shall have a new birth of freedom—and that government of the people, by the people, for the people, shall not perish from the earth."

In 1885 Miss Belle F. Keyes wrote Honorable Robert T. Lincoln asking him about this copy, then and still owned by the Keyes family, and he wrote her a letter which has been read in the Senate, but which only shows that Robert T. Lincoln at that date had no very exact knowledge of the origin or of the version of the address:

"Chicago, 16 Dec. 1885

"Dear Madame:

"It gives me pleasure to answer your inquiry. My father's Gettysburg Address was jotted down in pencil, in part, at least, on his way to the place. Mr. Everett expressed to him his gratification and upon his request my father wrote out the address in ink and sent it to him, and this is no doubt the copy you have. My father made another copy in ink to be used in getting a collection in lithographic copy called 'Autographic Leaves of our Country's

Authors' for the benefit of the great Sanitary Fair in Baltimore, and the facsimile is contained in a copy of the book which I have. I do not know of any other autographic copy nor what became of the original notes. They were probably used in delivering the address and then destroyed but as to that I have no knowledge.

"I am very truly yours,

"Robert T. Lincoln."

Mr. Robert T. Lincoln, though not knowing or professing to know very much about this matter either then or several years later when I had correspondence with him on the same subject, was correct in his belief that the copy in *Autograph Leaves* was the one made for the Baltimore Fair, and of that volume and the manuscript which Lincoln made for it we shall presently take account.

Lincoln did not devote very much of his time, comparatively speaking, to work upon his Gettysburg Address. Other matters were on his mind and demanded his attention. The war did not end. To be sure, there was progress, but it was wearisome and bloody. General Grant fought and won the battles of Missionary Ridge and Lookout Mountain. There Hooker distinguished himself, and raised anew the question whether he was not indeed a great General; but Grant said that while Hooker was a brilliant man, he was always considering some plan by which, instead of giving full and loyal cooperation to the plan of the commanding officer, he might detach a group of the younger officers and fight a battle of his own. Lincoln thought so, too. Hooker was commended but not placed at the head of an independent army again. General Thomas, slow but sure, fought and won at Franklin and Nashville and recovered middle and west Tennessee. General Sherman went on his march to the sea.

Lincoln was anxious about that, and so was Grant, for that matter, but it cut another wide swath through the heart of the Confederacy. General Grant came east and started in on the grim, remorseless business of grinding Lee's army to pieces. And he knew that his own army was to be terribly ground in the process. But two things were evident. One was that a war as long fought as that war had been must be brought to a definite end or the nation would be bankrupt by its continuance. The other was that Grant could afford to lose men in battle and could not afford to lose them by camp disease. Soldiers who die of camp fever are just as dead as those who die in battle, and their death does not advance the line. Grant lost more soldiers than Lee, and that was to be expected and could be afforded. The war must be fought to an end, and there was no gentle way to do it. The method was, as had been suggested to Lincoln, with one important modification, the old fight of the Kilkenny cats:

"There wanst was two cats in Kilkenny,
And aitch thought there was one cat too many;
　　So they quarreled and fit,
　　And they gouged and they bit,
　　Till excepting their nails,
　　And the tips of their tails,
Instead of two cats there war'nt any."

The important modification was, as Lincoln said, "Our cat has the longest tail."

He should have said "longer." But it was not wholly a matter of grammar; it was the stern business of attrition. Grant went at it in that way, and the losses of McClellan, Burnside, Hooker and the rest were small compared with his. But after every fight Lee's army was a little weaker in proportion, and the end of the war was a little nearer.

It was hard for a sympathetic man to see all this and approve it, but Lincoln did approve. It was, after all, the most merciful way to finish the war. But it was filling the hospitals.

The Baltimore Sanitary Fair, which, by the way, Mr. and Mrs. Lincoln attended in person, became the occasion of the final form of the address. Honorable George Bancroft asked for a copy of the manuscript, and Lincoln wrote it out with care in what we may call the fifth form. It differed very slightly from that which had been made for the New York Fair. The President wrote on the two sides of a single sheet. This made the copy unavailable for purposes of lithography, and Mr. Bancroft asked permission to retain it for himself, and requested the President to make a new copy, on one side only of the paper. The sixth and as far as is known the final copy was made by President Lincoln, March 11, 1864. He wrote with great care, and his writing filled two pages and ran a little way over on to a third. It was Lincoln's final and deliberate version.

To summarize and recapitulate:

Six times, at least, Lincoln wrote the Gettysburg Address in his own hand. Five of the autographs we have, and also an official and presumably accurate printing of the one missing manuscript.

The first, as I believe, was written mainly in Washington before Lincoln left for Gettysburg. The original is in the Library of Congress.

The second, in my opinion, was written in the house of Mr. Wills on the morning of the delivery of the address. This also, is in the Library of Congress.

The third was written a few days later, for the use of Mr. Wills in the official report. It is this of which we have no written original, and depend on the official printing of the report for the Governor of Pennsylvania. My conjecture is that in this version Lincoln simply amended a press report and that his secretaries copied it.

The fourth was written at the request of Honorable Edward Everett, for the New York Sanitary Fair. It is now owned by Honorable Henry W. Keyes, United States Senator from New Hampshire.

The fifth was prepared at the request of Honorable George Bancroft for use in the book entitled *Autograph Leaves of our Country's Authors.* As it was written on both sides of the paper it was unavailable. The original is in the possession of the Bancroft family.

The sixth and last is that which Lincoln made for the *Autograph Leaves,* copies of which were sold at the Sanitary Fair in Baltimore. It is unique in being on three pages, all the others being on two. The original is owned by William J. A. Bliss, of Baltimore.

Lincoln knew when he wrote his sixth and last known copy that the address was to be preserved in a volume with somewhat wide circulation. He had had several months in which to work over his material, and that in the light of the several reports that had been copied and prepared for him. His deliberate judgment should stand as to the precise form in which the Gettysburg Address ought to be remembered. This is what, after full deliberation, he wished he had said:

"Four score and seven years ago our fathers brought forth on this continent, a new nation, conceived in Liberty, and dedicated to the proposition that all men are created equal.

"Now we are engaged in a great civil war, testing whether that nation, or any nation so conceived and so dedicated, can long endure. We are met on a great battle-field of that war. We have come to dedicate a portion of that field, as a final resting place for those who here gave their lives that that nation might live. It is altogether fitting and proper that we should do this.

"But, in a larger sense, we can not dedicate—we can not consecrate—we can not hallow—this ground. The brave men, living and dead, who struggled here have consecrated it, far above our poor power to add or detract. The world will little note, nor long remember what we say here, but it can never forget what they did here. It is for us the living, rather, to be dedicated here to the unfinished work which they who fought here have thus far so nobly advanced. It is rather for us to be here dedicated to the great task remaining before us—that from these honored dead we take increased devotion to that cause for which they gave the last full measure of devotion—that we here highly resolve that these dead shall not have died in vain— that this nation, under God, shall have a new birth of freedom—and that government of the people, by the people, for the people, shall not perish from the earth."

CHAPTER XVI

THE WORLD LITTLE NOTED BUT LONG REMEMBERED

LINCOLN was an orator. Had he been everything else
that he was, a man of ability, character, patriotism and
honor, but had he not been an orator, he never could have
risen to the great height which he attained. The world
would little have noted nor long remembered what he said
if he had not had the power to move men by the living
voice. He would doubtless have been a worthy and useful
man without his gift of speech, but he could not thus have
accomplished what he did accomplish in life.

That being the case, it is interesting to record that the
Gettysburg Address did not succeed as oratory. All attempts of later students to make it appear that Lincoln
gained the sympathetic attention and emotional control of
his audience at Gettysburg, that he carried them with him
not only in intellectual accord but in spirit and feeling, fail
to convince us. He accepted the compliments of those who
gave him formal and measured praise, but these words did
not deceive him. He knew that people were curious to see
and hear the President, and that they were interested in
having seen and heard him, but he did not let himself believe that he had carried his audience with him as he had
used to do in the old days of outdoor campaign oratory.
It was a different occasion.

I am of the opinion that it is much to the credit of
Abraham Lincoln that he recognized the occasion as one in
which it would have been in bad taste for him to attempt

113

anything in the way of oratory, and that he is to be commended for having done the modest and, as it then appeared, the ineffective thing he did.

Be this as it may, it is as literature, not oratory, that the Gettysburg Address is to be judged. The first critical judgments published concerning it were not from the pens of those who heard it, but from those whose knowledge was limited to its appearance in print. From the beginning, its judgments have been based on literary, not oratorical criteria. And it is as literature the world must continue to judge of it, for whatever impression it made on human ears that heard it at Gettysburg, is now lost to us save as it reaches us through faint and not wholly consistent tradition.

What did the newspapers have to say about it at the time? For the most part the larger ones said nothing. Their comments were reserved for the great oration that had been delivered by Everett. Horace Greeley made no editorial comment in the *Tribune,* and neither did James Gordon Bennett in the *Herald,* or Henry J. Raymond in the *Times.* Later, both Greeley and Raymond admired it, but apparently they saw nothing in it until others called their attention to it. Thurlow Weed, of the Albany *Journal,* one of the most astute editors in his day, made no comment on the address, nor did Joseph Medill, of the Chicago *Tribune.* Some papers, of political faith opposed to that of the President, openly charged that he had desecrated the graves of Union soldiers by making a stump speech in the National Cemetery. One of the nearest important newspapers, the *Patriot and Union,* of Harrisburg, Pennsylvania, said:

"The President succeeded on this occasion because he acted without sense and without constraint in a panorama that was gotten up more for the benefit of his party than for the glory of the nation and the honor of the dead. . . . We pass over the silly remarks of the President; for the credit of the nation we are willing that the veil of oblivion shall be dropped over them and that they shall no more be repeated or thought of."

The Chicago *Times* and the *Register* in Lincoln's own home town of Springfield, and other partizan newspapers were equally caustic and equally unjust. Whatever is to be said of the Gettysburg speech, it certainly was not a political harangue.

But if the editors of the leading newspapers of America did not discover that the Gettysburg Address was a notable production, who did discover it?

The first favorable comment I have found was not an editorial judgment, but the enthusiastic comment of a reporter, and it was used next day in the Chicago *Tribune*. The present editors of that paper are unable to learn who was the author of the single sentence of commendation. Both the Chicago *Tribune* and the Chicago *Times* had reporters present. The *Times* of November twenty-first, reserving its bitter criticism for a special editorial, had only this comment:

"Our special telegraphic reporter furnishes a detailed account of the inauguration of the National Cemetery at Gettysburg. President Lincoln made a few remarks upon the occasion."

The *Tribune's* correspondent apparently could not obtain the wire in Gettysburg for a long account, but rode across to Harrisburg, writing as he rode, and his story appeared a day late, as did that of the *Times*. But the

Tribune correspondent wired from Gettysburg one sentence which appeared the day following the delivery of the address and may have been the first favorable comment published:

"The dedicatory remarks by President Lincoln will live among the annals of man."

This, I judge to have been the earliest printed expression of appreciation of the address; but it can not take rank as a mature and discriminating judgment.

It is often affirmed that the beauty of this address was first acknowledged in England. I have never been able to find the newspapers containing these alleged English expressions of approval. Few of these papers paid any attention to it. The London *Times* of December fourth gave an account of the dedication, and referred to the President's part in a paragraph, which, though written by the American correspondent of that journal, probably reflected the editorial attitude:

"The ceremony was rendered ludicrous by some of the sallies of that poor President Lincoln, who seems determined to play, in this great American union, the part of the famous Governor of Barataria. Anything more dull and commonplace it wouldn't be easy to produce."

On the other hand, a notable paragraph by Goldwin Smith appeared in *Macmillan's Magazine* for February, 1865, but that was fifteen months later, after a number of American editors had spoken well of the address:

"That Lincoln is something more than a boor his address at Gettysburg will in itself suffice to prove. There are one or two phrases here, such as 'dedicated to the proposition,' which betray a hand untrained in fine writing, and are proofs that the composition is Lincoln's own. But looking at the substance it may be doubted whether any king in Europe would have expressed himself more royally than the peasant's son. And even as to form we cannot help remarking that simplicity of structure and pregnancy of meaning are the true characteristics of the classical style. Is it easy to believe that the man who had the native good taste to produce this address would be capable of committing gross indecencies, that he would call for comic songs to be sung over soldiers' graves?"

Not reckoning the Chicago *Tribune* reporter's single sentence as an editorial comment, so far as I can learn, the first editorial comment which showed a discriminating appreciation of the Gettysburg Address as literature, appeared in the Springfield *Republican*. It might have been written by the editor, Samuel Bowles, but is more likely to have been the product of the pen of a member of the staff, Dr. J. G. Holland. Doctor Holland, in his *Life of Lincoln,* gave only a single sentence by way of comment on the Gettysburg Address, but what he said was essentially the same as it appeared in this editorial. It had no caption, but its emphasis was on the literary merit of the address:

"Surpassingly fine as Mr. Everett's oration was in the Gettysburg consecration, the rhetorical honors of the occasion were won by President Lincoln. His little speech is a perfect gem; deep in feeling, compact in thought and expression, and tasteful and elegant in every word and comma. Then it has the merit of unexpectedness in its verbal perfection and beauty. We had grown so accustomed to homely and imperfect phrase in his productions that we had come to think it was the law of his utterance. But this shows he can talk handsomely as well as act sensibly. Turn back and read it over, it will repay study as a model speech.   Strong feelings and a large brain were its parents—a little painstaking its accoucheur."

But while this editorial is cordial praise of the beauty and significance of the address, the present editor of the Springfield *Republican* in a recent editorial, in which the foregoing paragraph was printed by request, could not refrain from saying:

"Yet how illuminating is the editorial in revealing the contemporaneous view of the President!   The editorial writer knew that this was a 'perfect gem,' a 'model speech;' yet he was surprised that such verbal perfection and beauty should have come from Mr. Lincoln.   He had grown accustomed to 'homely and imperfect phrase' in the utterances of the President.   If the writer of this early appreciation of the Gettysburg address had entertained such an estimate of Mr. Lincoln's style, in what sort of esteem was it held by educated people in general?"

Two other eastern newspapers gave prompt recognition to the fine quality of Lincoln's speech.   The Providence *Journal* said:

"We know not where to look for a more admirable speech than the brief one which the President made at the close of Mr. Everett's oration.   It is often said that the hardest thing in the world is to make a five-minutes' speech. But could the most elaborate and splendid oration be more beautiful, more touching, more inspiring, than those thrilling words of the President?   They had in our humble judgment the charm and power of the very highest eloquence."

The *Evening Bulletin,* of Philadelphia, said:

Four score and seven years ago our fathers brought forth, upon this continent, a new nation, conceived in Liberty, and dedicated to the proposition that all men are created equal.

Now we are engaged in a great civil war, testing whether that nation, or any nation, so conceived, and so dedicated, can long endure. We are met here on a great battle-field of that war. We have come to dedicate a portion of it, as the final resting place for those who here gave their lives that that nation might live. It is altogether fitting and proper that we should do this.

But in a larger sense we can not dedicate— we can not consecrate— we can not hallow this ground. The brave men, living and dead, who struggled here, have consecrated it, far above our poor power to add or detract. The world will little note, nor long remember, what we say here, but can never forget what they did here. It is for us, the living, rather to be dedicated here to the unfinished work which they have, thus far, so nobly carried on. It is rather

The second autograph copy of the Gettysburg Address and the one which Lincoln held in his hand when he delivered the address. It was written in ink, on white paper, blue-lined, like that on which he had written the second page of the first draft. This was written in Gettysburg on the morning of the delivery of the address.

for us to be here dedicated to the great
task remaining before us— that from these
honored dead we take increased devotion
to that cause for which they here gave ~~o~~
the last full measure of devotion— that
we here highly resolve that these dead
shall not have died in vain; that this
nation shall have a new birth of freedom,
and that this government of the people, by
the people, for the people, shall not perish
from the earth.

"The President's brief speech of dedication is most happily expressed. It is warm, earnest, unaffected, and touching. Thousands who would not read the long, elaborate oration of Mr. Everett will read the President's few words, and not many will do it without a moistening of the eye and a swelling of the heart."

Neither the Detroit *Free Press,* an anti-administration organ, nor the *Advertiser and Tribune,* a strong supporter of Lincoln, had any report of the paragraph. The accounts when published were abbreviated. But on Monday, November twenty-third, the Detroit *Advertiser and Tribune* said in its leading editorial:

"The extended and elaborate oration of Mr. Everett will be widely read, and wherever it goes will nobly tell the story of those three heroic days at Gettysburg, and what is at stake in our stupendous struggle with rebellion. But he who wants to take in the very spirit of the day, catch the unstudied pathos that animates a sincere but simple-minded man, will turn from the stately periods of the professed orator to the brief speech of the President."

The Louisville *Journal* was already urging the name of General McClellan as the next President. It made no mention of the dedication of the cemetery, but contained a paragraph which was evidently suggested by the event. On November twenty-fourth, it said, editorially:

"Mr. Lincoln aspires to a second term in the Presidency. There are weighty considerations which should defeat this aspiration, and which we believe will defeat it. He has shown himself immensely destitute of the moral and intellectual fitness to exercise the limited authority the

Constitution gives him—much more to exercise the un-
limited authority he assumes. In this opinion we believe
so many of the loyal people of the Union concur, that Mr.
Lincoln's aspiration for a second term is destined to wither
under a killing frost."

Rather common was this view of Lincoln's appearance
at Gettysburg—he had taken that occasion to thrust himself before the nation as a candidate for reelection.

On the same day, the Louisville *Democrat,* which apparently had selected Governor Seymour, of New York, as
its candidate for the presidency, making no mention of
Gettysburg, said in an editorial paragraph:

"Mr. Lincoln is reported to have said that issuing the
Emancipation Proclamation is the greatest mistake of his
life. Mistake is a very mild term for it. The Cincinnati
Gazette asks if the Americans have lost confidence in
popular government. No, only in the present unpopular
government."

The Cincinnati *Commercial* had a report by a special
correspondent, and said, "The central figure is, of course
that of the orator, Mr. Everett." The Cincinnati *Gazette*
was warmly supporting President Lincoln. It gave a detailed account of the dedication, and printed Everett's address in full. It also had its own version of Lincoln's
address. But editorially it devoted its space to Everett,
and of Lincoln only said, "President Lincoln made a few
remarks."

The Missouri *Democrat,* a Union paper, printed
Everett's address in full on the front page, and gave
Lincoln's a very obscure place on the second page. The
Missouri *Republican,* an administration organ, said that

Lincoln's address was followed by "immense applause" and printed it, as it did Everett's, but without comment.

One of the earliest journalists to express appreciation of the Gettysburg Address was George William Curtis, editor of *Harper's Weekly*. In the issue of December 5, 1863, he said:

"The oration by Mr. Everett was smooth and cold. Delivered doubtless with his accustomed graces, it yet wanted one stirring thought, one vivid picture, one thrilling appeal.

"The few words of the President were from the heart to the heart. They cannot be read, even, without kindling emotion. 'The world will little note nor long remember what we say here, but it can never forget what they did here.' It was as simple and felicitous and earnest a word as was ever spoken."

And again, in the issue of April 23, 1864, the editor of *Harper's Weekly* wrote:

"Lieutenant-Colonel Alexander Bliss, of General Wallace's staff in Maryland, has prepared a unique and most valuable contribution to the Sanitary Fair, which is to open in Baltimore upon the 19th of April, a day of tragical interest in the history of the city . . . The book will be called 'Autograph Leaves of Our Country's Authors,' and will have a neat introduction by John P. Kennedy, author of 'Horse-Shoe Robinson,' and one of the stanchest of Maryland patriots, of course in fac-simile autograph. The two opening autographs of the volume, after the preface, are Key's 'Star-Spangled Banner' and President Lincoln's speech at Gettysburg, the most perfect piece of American eloquence, and as noble and pathetic and appropriate as the oration of Pericles over the Peloponnesian dead."

After Lincoln's death a number of ministers, however, did make reference to this speech. They did not refer to it familiarly as "the Gettysburg address," nor assume that their congregation had it in mind. They spoke of it as "the few remarks" with which the President followed "the eloquent address" of Edward Everett. They all spoke of it in terms of appreciation, and at least one of them, Reverend John McClintock, cited it as evidence of Lincoln's intellectual power. Almost if not quite invariably, the use they made of it was to urge upon their congregations a dedication of themselves to the uncompleted task for which Lincoln had given his life. Neither they nor their congregations had become familiar with it, or accustomed to thinking of it as a great address. Only here and there was there discernment of its fine character. The real discovery of the high merit of the Gettysburg Address came gradually, and much later, and belongs to no one discoverer.

It is of interest to inquire what reference was made to the Gettysburg Address in the sermons preached throughout the country on the Sunday immediately following the death of Lincoln, or on one of the Sundays immediately succeeding. Reference has already been made to the sermon of Reverend D. T. Carnahan, of Gettysburg, which was full of praise for Lincoln, but contained no suggestion that Lincoln had ever been in Gettysburg, no allusion to the address as something which the people of the congregation had heard and remembered.

If to any reader the foregoing paragraph appears to pass the bounds of credibility, it may be of interest to him to know that it made the same impression on the proof-reader, who wrote in the margin of the first proofs that the statement that Mr. Carnahan made no allusion to the Gettysburg Address seemed incredible. The author thereupon read the address again, and with increased appreciation of its quality. Mr. Carnahan was a man of education and of sound judgment, and his oration, for so it was entitled, was prepared with long and patient care. It paid a very high tribute to the deceased President, and Mr. Carnahan evidently felt that he needed some words of Lincoln's own to justify his description. He found those words in Lincoln's address to his old neighbors as he was leaving Springfield, and quoted it in full as proof of the President's greatness and goodness; he made no reference to Lincoln's visit to Gettysburg or to the Gettysburg Address!

As far as I could learn, no one in Gettysburg thought that Mr. Carnahan had omitted anything of importance. The local paper uttered no protest. It announced that Mr. Carnahan's address was in print; that it was an eloquent oration, and that it could be had for ten cents a copy at certain places in Gettysburg, and that every one ought to read it; all of which was true. But the same issue that carried this recommendation of the Carnahan oration had a column story of the Emancipation Proclamation, and not a syllable about the fact that Abraham Lincoln had ever visited Gettysburg! Could anything be more significant of the feeling of those who heard Lincoln's immortal words? Later, of course, they all remembered that they thought from the beginning that his was a great speech. If anybody in Gettysburg thought so at the time, he kept far away from the printing press. Gettysburg little noted, but long afterward remembered, what he said there.

CHAPTER XVII

AFTER TWO GENERATIONS

ABRAHAM LINCOLN delivered addresses which, even as read at this distance, display the power of the true orator; but the speeches that made him famous, those that displayed his power to inform the mind, convince the reason, sway the passions and determine the action of his audiences, are little read now. The world did not fail to note but it does not now remember his real orations. That part of the world that listened to his "lost speech" at Bloomington, his State Fair speech at Springfield, his Peoria address and his Cooper Union masterpiece was deeply moved by his utterance; but these orations now, in thick volumes diligently perused by the special student, are, for the general reader, "folioed and forgot." Abraham Lincoln never suspected that almost the only scrap of oratory by which the world would remember him would be his Gettysburg Address.

Abraham Lincoln said at Gettysburg, "The world will little note nor long remember what we say here, but it can never forget what they did here." He was never more mistaken in all his life. The men who fought on that red field did more than they knew while they were fighting; more than they understood after they had won the victory. They did more even than Lincoln realized four months later as he stood on the spot and paid tribute to their sacrifice. But memorable as were the deeds they wrought there, the world will longer remember the words he spoke there. The Gettysburg Address will be printed and recited

and translated and cast in durable bronze long after it shall
have become necessary to append foot-notes to explain that
Gettysburg was neither a battle in the Revolutionary War,
nor a field somewhere amid the poppies of Flanders. Deeds
are memorable, but words rightly chosen and well spoken
are immortal.

> "We and the gods depart,
> And all things else except the Word."

And yet at the time it seemed wholly possible that
Lincoln's statement might be literally true. The world
appeared not to note the words he uttered, and it is not
certain that a majority of those who heard him expected
that what he said would be long remembered. The auditors
saw the President, whom most of them had never seen
before; they heard him in his brief and subordinate part
in an important celebration; so much they were not likely
to forget; but not all of them thought his words to be
significant. No one doubts their significance now.

Many of the battle-fields of the Civil War are almost
forgotten. Bull Run is a place of farms and forests. Shiloh
is as desolate as the site of the ancient sanctuary whose
name it bears. Appomattox has been reconquered by the
wilderness. But Gettysburg lives. Vicksburg, fought on
the same days, can be and is declared by competent military
authorities to have been more notable as a battle and more
significant as a victory than Gettysburg; it certainly is not
of negligible importance in comparison with the latter;
but Vicksburg is not a place of pilgrimage as Gettysburg is.
Innumerable paths lead the tourist and the imagination to
Gettysburg. What makes Gettysburg immortal is less the
military victory than the speech of Lincoln. His words
already serve to give immortality to memorable deeds. The

world has nearly forgotten what brave men did on many
another battle-field of the war that saved the Union and
overthrew slavery, but not Gettysburg. The world remembers longer and more vividly what they did there
because it so definitely remembers what he said there.

This would have surprised Abraham Lincoln. When
he said that what he was saying would soon be forgotten,
he uttered a prediction as honest as it was modest. Any
prophecy widely at variance with that sentiment would
have offended his hearers. They supposed themselves to
be hearing a scrap of somewhat perfunctory oratory, important only because it was spoken by the President of the
United States. And he, whatever opinion we form as to
his own estimate of his utterance, never suspected that his
words would live as they have lived and are to live.

Several eminent critics have compared the Gettysburg
Address with the Funeral Oration of Pericles. The editor
of an American newspaper published in the Greek language
has recently made this theme the basis of an interesting
comparison. Dr. Charles Moore says it was George William Curtis who first noted this supposed resemblance, and
Doctor Moore quotes from Thucydides in the Perrin
translation the following paragraph:

"It is hard for a speaker to observe due moderation
in a case where his hearer can scarcely be made to cherish a
proper conception of the truth. For the hearer who is
acquainted with the facts and well disposed toward the
dead, will possibly deem the setting forth of praise all too
sparing in the light of his desires and knowledge; while he
who is without knowledge in the case will suspect exagger-
ation here and there, because he is jealous on hearing of
aught that surpasses his own powers. Men tolerate the
praises of other men only so far as they think themselves

capable, every one, of performing the deeds recited to them; but when such deeds are beyond them they are jealous at once and incredulous."

For myself, I have never been able to discover the alleged similarities of thought between Lincoln and Pericles or Thucydides. I am rather sorry. I think I could easily find analogies between Everett and the orations of classical Greece, but I do not find them in Lincoln, here or elsewhere. I merely print the statements of those who think they have discovered them, as George William Curtis and others thought themselves able to do. To me, Lincoln's utterances seem cast in a very different mold.

One of the most discriminating and just of all tributes to the Gettysburg Address, including as it should a tribute also to the Second Inaugural, is to be found in the Rede Lecture, by Lord Curzon, Earl of Kedleston, Chancellor of the University of Oxford, delivered before the University of Cambridge, November 6, 1913, on "Modern Parliamentary Eloquence." Speaking of the decline of eloquence of modern parliamentary bodies, and raising the question whether that decline was to be regarded as temporary or permanent, he assured his hearers that eloquence could not possibly have taken its final leave of parliamentary bodies. He said:

"Just as the oratory of the Georgian era was attuned to an aristocratic age, and that of the Victorian epoch to the middle-class ascendancy, so does it seem to me likely that democracy will produce an eloquence, even an oratory of its own. Should a man arise from the ranks of the people, as Abraham Lincoln from the back-woods of America, a man gifted with real oratorical power, and with commanding genius, I can see no reason why he should not revive in England the glories of a Chatham or a Gratton. His triumphs might be less in the Senate than in the arena; his style might not be that of the classics of the past. But he might by reason of his gifts climb to the topmost place, where he would sway the destinies of the State, and affect the fortunes of an empire."

Lord Curzon's closing paragraphs contain an even finer tribute to Lincoln. He felt that the character of his own address had been such, surveying as he did in outline the history of British parliamentary oratory, that he might be expected to designate what he regarded "as the supreme masterpiece." He found three famous modern orations of which he said that "they emerge with a superiority which, if not disputable, will perhaps not be seriously disputed. These three," he said, "are preeminent, much as the 'Funeral Oration' of Pericles was generally allowed to be the master-piece of the ancient world." These three "supreme master-pieces" of English eloquence, he declared, were the toast of William Pitt after the victory at Trafalgar, and two of Lincoln's speeches: the Gettysburg Address and the Second Inaugural.

That Lord Curzon should have come to America for two of these three masterpieces was highly complimentary to the oratory of this country. But it was even more significant that both of these addresses should have been by Abraham Lincoln. Of them he said:

"They were uttered by a man who had been a country farmer and a district lawyer before he became a statesman. But they are among the glories and treasures of mankind. I escape the task of deciding which is the masterpiece of modern English eloquence by awarding the prize to an American.

"The Gettysburg Address is far more than a pleasing piece of occasional oratory. It is a marvelous piece of English composition. It is a pure well of English undefiled. It sets one to inquiring with nothing short of wonder 'How knoweth this man letters, having never learned?' The more closely the address is analyzed the more one must confess astonishment at its choice of words, the precision of its thought, its simplicity, directness and effectiveness.

"But it is more than an admirable piece of English composition, it is an amazingly comprehensive and forceful presentation of the principles for which the war then was waging. It was a truthful recital of the events which lay behind the gathering at Gettysburg, and an interpretation of the spirit of the occasion. It joined the local to the national, the occasional to the permanent; it went straight at a declaration of the purpose which animated the soul of Abraham Lincoln, and for which the men buried at Gettysburg had given their lives. Above all it was a declaration of America's fundamental principles. It truthfully represented the spirit of that for which men fought, not only at Gettysburg but at Runnymeade, at Bunker Hill, and on the plains of Flanders. The long, hard fought battle for the liberation of humanity has been a struggle for the rights and welfare of humanity."

CHAPTER XVIII

Sources of the Gettysburg Address

The first evident source of the Gettysburg Address is the little speech of President Lincoln on Tuesday evening, July 7, 1863. This has already been dealt with and need not here be elaborated. The transition from "eighty-odd years since" to "four score and seven years ago" is hardly less than an inspiration. A recent attempt has been made to derive this phrase from A. B. Meek, of Memphis, in an address of welcome to returned soldiers from the Mexican War. Speaking at Mobile, Alabama, July 4, 1848, he is alleged to have said: "Three score years and ten and two have passed since the establishment of her nationality by the Declaration of Independence."* But this is too casual and incidental a resemblance to indicate a probable connection.

Lincoln himself is the first and most important source of the address, and we are able to trace to some degree its evolution, beginning with his little response to the belated fourth of July serenade.

Another important source was the address of Edward Everett. Lincoln's reading of the proofs of this masterly effort did not lead him into any futile attempt at imitation whether of style, length or method; yet no one can read the two papers and remember that Lincoln had perused

---

*"National Welcome to the Soldiers Returning from Mexico; an Oration Delivered at Mobile, Alabama, July 4, 1848." In *Romantic Passages in Southwestern History*, Mobile and New York, S. F. Goetzel & Co., 1857.

the address of Everett and not be impressed with a similarity of thought. Lincoln's originality of treatment is nowhere more in evidence. The words are his own; the style is his own; the logic is his own; yet the kinship of thought is beyond question.

The most interesting question concerning Lincoln's sources, is, where did he get the phrase "government of the people, by the people, for the people"?

It has been charged that he took it bodily from Daniel Webster. John T. Morse, Jr., by a singular and wholly needless blunder, quotes the Gettysburg Address in full and then adds this amazing bit of information:

"It is, perhaps, not generally remembered that Mr. Lincoln added to the words which he himself had written a quotation of one of Daniel Webster's most famous flights of oratory,—that familiar passage is the reply to Hayne, beginning: 'When my eyes turn to behold for the last time the sun in heaven,' etc. The modesty was better than the skill of this addition; the simplicity of the President's language and the elevation of the sentiment which it expressed did not accord well with the more rhetorical enthusiasm of Webster's outburst. The two passages, each so fine in its own way, were incongruous in their juxtaposition."

Mr. Morse was correct in his statement that this borrowing from Webster was "not generally remembered;" it would have been better if Mr. Morse had not remembered it. His book, in some respects a good one, is seriously marred by errors like this. But the words which Lincoln actually said, and which Morse quoted and therefore did not refer to in the foregoing paragraph, were near enough to an utterance of Webster's that the latter might have suggested the expression to Lincoln. It occurred in Webster's second speech on the Foot Resolution, January 26, 1830, his famous reply to Hayne, and that was one of the documents which Lincoln studied before, in preparation for his First Inaugural. Webster defined the American government as

"The people's government, made for the people, made by the people, and answerable to the people."

Many authorities have declared that Lincoln got the phrase from the Introduction to Wycliff's Bible. I have had the Wycliff Bibles in the Library of Congress and in the New York Public Library searched and this phrase has not been found. The Congregational Library of Boston has a notable collection of Bibles, and the librarian furnishes me the following note, which is in accord with what I have also by the courtesy of the New York and Washington librarians:

"I have looked through the preface and prologue of our edition of Wycliffe's Bible, and I do not find the quotation, 'This Bible is for the government of the people, by the people, and for the people.'

"The same thought runs however, through the following extract, which may give you a little assistance:

" 'Lord God! Sithen at the bigynnyng of feith so manie men translatiden into Latyn, and to greet profyt of Latyn men, lat oo symple creature of God translate into English, for profyt of English men; for it worldli clerkis loken wel here croniclis and bokis, thei shulden fynde, that Bede translatide the bible, and expounide myche in Saxon, that was English, either comoun langage of this lond, in his tyme; and not oneli Bede, but also king Alured, that foundied Oxenford, translatide in hise laste daies the begynnyng of the Sauter into Saxon, and wolde more, if he hadde lyved longere.   Also Frenshe men, Beemers, and Britons have the bible, and othere bokis of denocioun and of exposicioun, translatid in here modir langage; whi shulden not English men have the same in here modin langage.   I can not wite, no but for falsnesse and necgligence of clerkis, either for oure puple is not worthi to have so greet grace and gifte of God, in peyne of here olds synnes.   God for his merci amende these enele causis, and make oure puple to have, and kunne, and kepe truli holi writ, to lyf and deth!' "

A still earlier origin of the idea has been suggested in an address by Cleon, a tanner by trade, who in the year 420 B.C., is alleged to have said to the men of Athens:

"I am in favor of the democracy that shall be democratic, that shall give us the rule, which shall be of the people, by the people, for the people."

So the words may be as old as Pericles!

Indeed, we are reminded that Pericles in a memorial address over Athenians who had fallen in battle said words strikingly like some that Lincoln uttered at Gettysburg. Pericles called upon the Athenians to dedicate and consecrate themselves anew in the light of the sacrifice of their fellow citizens, and used the words "nobly resolve."

Several foreign writers appear to have used the thought in modern times.   At a public meeting at Olten, Switzerland, in 1830, a citizen named Schintz is reputed to have said:

"All the government of Switzerland must acknowledge that they are simply from the people, by the people, and for the people."

In Lamertine's *History of the Girondists,* published in 1850, in a discussion of the theories of Robespierre, the words occur, as defining the end for which that statesman wrought:

"We preach Democracy in vain while Tory and Conservative can point to the opposite side of the Atlantic and say: 'There are nineteen millions of the human race free absolutely, every man heir to the throne, governing themselves—the government of all, by all, for all: but instead of being a consistent republic it is one widespread confederacy of free men for the enslavement of a nation of another complexion.' "

The earliest use of these or similar words in America may have been by John Adams:

"The declaration that our People are hostile to a government made by ourselves, for themselves, and conducted by themselves, is an insult."*

The idea was employed once by Honorable John Marshall:

"The government of the Union, then, is emphatically and truly a government of the people. In form and in substance it emanates from them. Its powers are granted by them, and are to be exercized directly on them and for their benefit."†

Address to the Citizens of Westmoreland Co., Virginia. Answered July 11, 1798. See also Thomas Cooper, *Some Information Respecting America* (1794). In *Report of a Meeting of the Massachusetts Historical Society,* by Samuel A. Green, May 9, 1901.

†Chief Justice Marshall. *Case of McCulloch vs. Maryland.* 1819. 4. Wheaton. 316.

geous ensign of the republic, now known and honored throughout the earth, stand full high advanced, its arms and trophies streaming in their original luster, not a stripe erased or polluted, not a single star obscured, bearing for its motto no such miserable interrogatory as 'What is all this worth?' nor those other words of delusion and folly, 'Liberty first and Union afterwards,' but everywhere, spread over all in characters of living light blazing on all its ample folds, as they float over the sea and over the land, and in every wind under the whole heavens, that other sentiment, dear to every true American heart—Liberty *and* Union, now and forever, one and inseparable!"

Lincoln believed with Webster that liberty and union were one and inseparable; beyond reasonable doubt these very words were among those that helped him define that conviction. But now another question rises, Where did Webster get the dignified figures of speech which made this closing period of his address the noblest of all his perorations? Apparently he found his thought in Milton's *Paradise Lost.*

In Milton's stupendous poem, Azazel, Satan's flag-bearer, having been cast down from heaven together with his lord and all attendant fallen angels, is first to rise out of the despair of their expulsion, and to lift the standard of revolt against high heaven. It is a terrible picture which Milton painted but one to inspire admiration. Partly by contrast, but not wholly so, Webster found in this description some aspects of his vision of a stainless and glorious flag, floating in triumph over a united country. We note the use of the word "ensign," the "luster" of its folds, the "arms and trophies" which accompany it. These in Milton's lines appear in Webster's oration. The poet describes the host that fell with Satan, and goes on:

"All these and more came flocking; but with looks
Downcast and damp; yet such wherein appeared
Obscure some glimpse of joy to have found their Chief
Not in despair, to have found themselves not lost
In loss itself; which on his countenance cast
Like doubtful hue. But he, his wonted pride
Soon recollecting, with high words, that bore
Semblance of worth, not substance, gently raised
Their fainted courage, and dispelled their fears:
Then straight commands that, at their warlike sound
Of trumpets loud and clarions, he upreared
His mighty standard. That proud honour claimed
Azazel as his right, a Cherub tall:
Who forthwith from the glittering staff unfurled
The imperial ensign; which full high advanced,
Shone like a meteor streaming to the wind,
With gems and golden lustre rich imblazed,
Seraphic arms and trophies; all the while
Sonorous metal blowing martial sounds:
At which the universal host up-sent
A shout that tore Hell's conclave, and beyond
Frighted the reign of Chaos and old Night."

It is interesting to inquire the source of Lincoln's most
important interpolation. When we compare the two forms
of the address which Lincoln wrote before he delivered it
with all the press reports and with his own revisions this
change confronts us. It is the words "under God." It is
the most notable variation in his address, and it calls for
extended consideration.

Neither of the drafts of Lincoln's manuscript made
before the delivery of the address contains the two words
"under God." Both say, "that we here highly resolve . . .
that the nation shall have a new birth of freedom." But
every stenographic report, good, bad and indifferent, says
"that the nation shall, under God, have a new birth of freedom." There was no common source from which all the

reporters could have obtained those words but from Lincoln's own lips at the time of delivery. It will not do to say that Stanton suggested those words after Lincoln's return to Washington, for the words were telegraphed by at least three reporters on the afternoon of delivery and printed all over the country. Nor will it answer to say that Seward suggested them the night before as words that would convey to the people assembled a suggestion of piety, for John G. Nicolay gives a clear history of the writing of the second draft on the morning of delivery and the second draft does not include those words. There is no evidence for, or help in, the hypothesis of Major Lambert that Lincoln had inadvertently left one draft of his speech in Washington. Lincoln was not the man to have left so important a document, and the hypothesis does not explain this significant change.

Where, then, did Lincoln get those words? He got them, I think, out of his own stock of phraseology. He was not given to the careless use of religious phrases, but this one he used at other times. It came to him as he sat on the platform at Gettysburg, inspired by the sense of solemnity that the occasion brought upon him. The journey, the reception of the night before, the parade, the sight of the battle-field, the long and eloquent oration of Edward Everett, and the growing depth of feeling as his own time came to speak, roused in him a deeper sense of the nation's need of reliance on God than had been in his mind when he was engaged in the work of writing. He said "under God" then and there because it was then and there borne in upon him that the nation must rely on God. And he said it because he felt it. Every orator who prepares his addresses in writing and delivers them without being closely confined to his manuscript knows that there come to him while on his feet, under the emotional stress of the occasion, expressions which no amount of cold thought would have enabled him to invent. That was the case with Lincoln.

But Lincoln could not have invented it if he had not had it already in his subconscious mind. It was not a court-room phrase. It was not a grouping of words which came back to him out of a legal argument. But it was a form of words not new to Lincoln; words do not thus come newly out of the void. Out of what quarry did Lincoln obtain the words "under God"?

It is more than possible that Lincoln got these words from Parson Weems. This gentleman who wrote *The Life of George Washington; with Curious Anecdotes, Equally Honourable to Himself, and Exemplary to His Young Countrymen,* has become the butt of the present generation, but he was no joke to the young Abraham Lincoln. Lincoln borrowed this book from his neighbor, named Crawford, and as it was damaged while in his possession, he had to pull fodder for three days at twenty-five cents a day to pay for it. How he read that book, and how indelible an impression it made upon him, we know from Lincoln's address before the Legislature at Trenton, in February, 1861. There he related how that book had thrilled him in his boyhood, and given him his best idea of the heroism not only of Washington but of the men of the Revolution who made America free.

It did not distress the young Lincoln that the boy George Washington and his father conversed together in preposterously stilted language in the pages of the Reverend Mason L. Weems. That was the way people were supposed to talk in books. The devotees of grand opera make the same mental accommodations when the heroes of that equally preposterous presentation strut their conversation. That is the way they are expected to do in grand opera, and the boy Abraham Lincoln was not in the least

Photo by W. H. Tipton

View of the peach orchard and wheat field

disturbed that they did something similar in lesser pomp in the pages of a book. He read Weems's *Life of Washington* with profit, and truth to tell, it is not quite so absurd a book as its modern critics say it is. It did Abraham Lincoln good, and he absorbed the book and remembered it all his life.

Lincoln had a good verbal memory. Phrases stuck in his mind, and he used them when he had occasion. He built up his vocabulary from his early reading of the Bible, *The Pilgrim's Progress, Robinson Crusoe* and a very few other good books, including, as we know, Weems's *Life of Washington*.

Now, "under God" was a favorite phrase of Parson Weems, and so far as I know it was not a phrase which Abraham Lincoln is likely to have encountered in any of his other reading. I am not sure that any other book that he ever owned contained these words. It may be well to cite some of Weems's uses of the phrase.

Mr. Weems related in detail the anxiety which Washington suffered while President, through the demands of France that America should stand ready on all occasions to fight France's battles. "Scarcely had Washington got clear of his embarrassments with Britain, before still worse were thrown in his way by France." That is a mild statement. The French embarrassment continued into the next administration, and Washington offered to John Adams to lead an invading army into France. Weems tells how this exasperating situation was permitted to go on longer than would otherwise have been tolerated, because the American people felt a deep and, perhaps, excessive gratitude to France, as "a beloved nation, to whom, under God, they owed their liberties."

That was the manner of his use of the term, with a recognition of human agency and divine Providence in supervision. And that was the way Lincoln used the phrase.

Mr. Weems uses the phrase again in his account of the impression made upon the country by the Farewell Address of George Washington. He says that the retirement of Washington, with a reference to the probable approach before many years of his own death, "struck everywhere a damp on the spirits of the people. To be thus bidden farewell by one to whom, in every time of danger, they had so long and so fondly looked up, as, under God, their surest and safest friend, could not but prove to them a grievous shock."

In his chapter on the death of Washington, he grows dramatic, and calls on the readers to assemble in imagination and behold as an impressive spectacle the dying of this great man:

"Sons and daughters of Columbia, gather yourselves together around the bed of your expiring father—around the last bed of him to whom you and your children owe, under God, many of the best blessings of this life."

Abraham Lincoln in his boyhood read that passage, and in imagination stood by the death-bed of Washington. He was not permitted to think that Washington had performed his great task unaided. He remembered that most vividly as he was leaving Springfield, to undertake, as he said, a task greater than that of Washington. He reminded himself and his neighbors that Washington could not have succeeded but for his trust in an overruling God, and he asked his neighbors to pray to Washington's God on his behalf. He knew that what Washington did, he did "under God."

Parson Weems was far from being the only man who ascribes to George Washington a divine call and mission, or who, in attributing to him qualities dangerously near to being superhuman, made verbally some recognition of Providence in the winning of America's independence. But I do not recall any of his contemporaries who habitually used this form of words "under God." And remembering Parson Weems's predilection for high-sounding words, I wonder that he said it so simply. Other men said that George Washington, in fulfillment of the high behest of heaven, fought and won our independence; or that George Washington heeding the divine call became the deliverer of his people from the British yoke; or that George Washington, in the providence of God, or, in pursuance of the will of God, fought and governed as he did. As far as I can recall my reading of the literature that followed the death of Washington, those were more nearly the forms of words employed, and something of the same, though perhaps with somewhat more of verbosity, characterized the oratory of the period. I am not rash enough to say that no one used this phrase except Parson Weems; I am only saying that I do not recall it in any other book that Lincoln would have been likely to read, and it was plainly a phrase that habitually flowed from the pen of Washington's first biographer. Mr. Weems was a boisterously patriotic man, and a vociferously religious man. It belonged to his view of the governance of the world to make provision for an acknowledgment of the will of God wrought out in human action. So he said, and said repeatedly, that great and good things were done by George Washington, and others, "under God." It was his favorite expression, and Lincoln inherited it.

It is notable that the expression "under God" was not unfamiliar to Washington himself, and we can but wonder if he, as well as Lincoln, got it from Parson Weems. On July 2, 1776, the very day the Declaration of Independence was approved by Congress, Washington summoned his men on Long Island to prepare to resist Lord Howe, whose ships then lay at anchor off Staten Island. He said:

"The fate of unknown millions will now depend, under God, on the courage and conduct of this army. Our cruel and unrelenting enemy leave us no choice but a brave resistance, or the most abject submission; this is all we can expect."*

That Lincoln owed a debt to Weems, he knew and acknowledged. That he realized himself to have been indebted to Weems for this form of words may not be so certain. Men do not always or perhaps usually remember where their happy phrases come from. Perhaps if Lincoln had been told that his phrase at Gettysburg was somewhat unusual, and had been asked where he picked it up, he could not have told. It has been common enough, of course, since Lincoln's day; he made it popular. It was not so common before.

This was not Lincoln's only use of the term, but this is what he said in his closing sentence at Gettysburg:

"It is rather for us to be here dedicated to the great task remaining before us—that from these honored dead we take increased devotion to that cause for which they gave the last full measure of devotion—that we here highly resolve that these dead shall not have died in vain—that this nation, *under God,* shall have a new birth of freedom— and that government of the people, by the people, for the people, shall not perish from the earth."

*Ford, *Writings of George Washington,* IV, 200, 202.

CHAPTER XIX

Analysis of the Gettysburg Address

The exact number of words in the Gettysburg Address varies with the version used and the method of counting. If the compound words "battle-field" and "resting-place" be counted as two words each, the six versions which Lincoln wrote give the following totals: first draft, 239; second draft, 269; third draft, 267; fourth draft, 273; fifth draft, 272; sixth draft, 272.

Of the two hundred and seventy-two words, counting repetitions, Lincoln five times used a word of one letter, the article "a"; he used forty-six words of two letters and fifty-four of three letters, fifty-six of four letters, thirty of five letters, twenty-five of six, thirteen of seven and the rest of eight or more. Lincoln used large words when he needed them, and used them with intelligence and precision; but mainly he employed short words.

This fact becomes the more apparent when we count the syllables. There are two hundred and four words of a single syllable each, fifty of two syllables and only eighteen of three or more.

Colonel Clark E. Carr, who more than once described and recited the address in my hearing, and whose testimony I rank highest of all among those with whom I have conversed on the subject, counted that, including repetitions, forty-six of the words used by Lincoln were of Latin derivation and two hundred twenty-six Anglo-Saxon. Only one-fifth of the words were other than plain old English.

145

Colonel Carr also noted that short as the address was, it contained all the elements of an elaborate and finished oration, as clearly defined in Lincoln's address as in that of Everett, which was definitely formed on classic models.

There is an exordium of five simple sentences, clear, direct, and so obvious that they might have seemed commonplace, but they lay deep and strong the foundations for the address.

Then follows the argument in five sentences, rising to a climax.

Then comes the peroration in a single sentence.

The Gettysburg Address has always had its critics. Matthew Arnold is declared to have read as far as "dedicated to the proposition" and have stopped there. I have never been able to discover on what evidence this statement rests. It might be admitted, however, that contrasted with "conceived in Liberty" the phrase "dedicated to the proposition" leaves something to be desired. I should not like to undertake to improve the Gettysburg Address, but as Lincoln rewrote it several times and each time improved it, there is a possibility that he might have thought of a better phrase than "dedicated to the proposition."*

If Seward or some other friend had gone over the Gettysburg Address in advance, as Seward did the First Inaugural, and had said to Lincoln that the adjective "great" is a pitfall for American orators, who tend too much to think of bulk, and who might with profit use other

---

*Professor John Erskine was quoted recently as saying that Matthew Arnold had criticized this phraseology. In a letter to the author Professor Erskine says:

"It was perhaps a mistake for me to repeat the statement that Matthew Arnold objected to the 'dedicated to the proposition,' for there is no written proof that he made this criticism. The criticism was repeated to me, however, by men who claim they had it from him when he was on his American tour. In the English Department here in Columbia, one of my colleagues, Arnold Whitridge, is, as you know, Arnold's grandson. Whitridge says that he has never seen this opinion of his grandfather's in print, but he has heard the opinion mentioned frequently."

adjectives a part of the time and with finer discrimination, perhaps Lincoln would have thought well not to say "a great civil war" and "a great battle-field." One use of that adjective, he might have thought sufficient.

If Lincoln had reviewed his speech more deliberately he might have become convinced that it was unfortunate to use the word "that" as many as thirteen times:

1.   *That* all men are created equal.
2.   Testing whether *that* nation . . . can long endure.
3.   A great battle-field of *that* war.
4.   To dedicate a portion of *that* field.
5.-6. Gave their lives *that that* nation might live.
7.   Altogether fitting and proper *that* we should do this.
8.   *That* from these honored dead.
9.   *That* cause for which they gave.
10.   *That* we here highly resolve.
11.   *That* these dead shall not have died in vain.
12.   *That* this nation under God shall have a new birth of freedom.
13.   *That* government of the people, by the people, for the people shall not perish from the earth.

As Lincoln used the word "that" in the Gettysburg Address it was employed variously, and that fact saved something of the otherwise inevitable monotony; but possibly if he had thought of it he could have substituted other words in a few instances.

A critic would probably say that it would have been better rhetorically if the word "devotion" had not been repeated in the sentence which contains it twice.

Lincoln had obvious trouble with his last sentence. Many orators fail completely there. He had a noble idea. It was almost too large for exact grammar. St. Paul had precisely the same difficulty in closing his epistle to the Romans. The thought with which he wished to conclude was

too great for language; it is not grammatical either in the
Greek text or in the English translations. And here is the
contrast between St. Paul and Abraham Lincoln on the one
hand and a majority of orators on the other. Mediocre
writers and speakers come to their close with nothing left
for a climax; St. Paul and Abraham Lincoln came to their
perorations each with an idea so vast its author struggled in
pain to give it birth. It is hardly likely that Lincoln would
have consented to cut up his closing sentences into others as
short as those with which he began. But his penciled emen-
dation at the bottom of the first sheet in the first draft is
documentary evidence of the trouble he had with it, and it
is not impossible he might have improved it. He would be
a brave man who would now undertake it.

There is no vindictiveness in the Gettysburg Address;
no hurling of defiance at the foe driven back from that
place; no appeal to passion against those whose invasion
of that peaceful spot had cost these lives. There is no
hate, no bitterness, no attempt to rouse passion. And there
is no apparent effort to keep these elements out of the
speech; they are not in the address because they were not in
the heart of Lincoln.

There is no suggestion in the Gettysburg Address that
this was the field on which might be erected a "high water
mark tablet" to indicate the point from which the red wave
of war was thenceforth to recede and never return. Lincoln hoped, no doubt, that the Confederate armies were
never to return that way, but so he had hoped after Antietam. He could not know that Pickett would never lead
another charge against the stone wall that broke his superb
column. Lincoln had to wait another year and more before
he could have said that with assurance. Had he known it,
the war was settled when it was decided that Lee could not
accomplish a successful invasion of the North. Very near

to the spot where he uttered his memorable words, the
thunders of war uttered the decrees of Providence that government of the people, by the people, and for the people,
should not perish from the earth.

In no one of the forms in which it is preserved, and in
no report of the address as it was delivered, did Lincoln
employ in the Gettysburg speech the pronoun "I." Probably it cost Lincoln no thought or self-denial to omit it.
Presumably he found no occasion to use it. He was not un-
accustomed to say "I." He could do it when there was
need. It simply did not occur to him, and the address would
not have been improved by its use.

The employment of the pronoun "I" is not a necessary
indication of egoism. And it is no charge of that character
which would be implied in a reminder that other Presidents
would certainly have used it. But very few Presidents
would have gone to Gettysburg and made a speech and gone
away and never once publicly have said "I."

I once undertook to rewrite the Gettysburg Address in
the style of Theodore Roosevelt and also in that of Wood-
row Wilson, and was rather pleased with my success. I will
not reproduce the results in this place; any one who likes
may try his hand at it. I was quite certain that both of these
men would have said "I." Roosevelt might have said, "I
propose that we here dedicate ourselves," and Wilson might
have said, "May I not suggest that we here highly resolve,"
but in some characteristic form, and one not inherently im-
modest, I thought that they certainly would have done it,
each in his own way.

Wilson did actually deliver a Gettysburg address. When
the semi-centennial celebration of the battle was planned, it
was intended to have four days' celebration, of which the
first three days should be of historical and commemorative
character, and the fourth day should be given up to a cele-

bration in which patriotism should be the theme, with an address by the President of the United States as its main feature. The President declined the invitation, giving as one of his reasons that he did not wish to invite a comparison of his address with that of Lincoln. I was informed at Gettysburg that this seemed to the Committee a needlessly self-conscious reply; and they reshaped the program, practically closing the celebration with the three historic days. But just before the celebration the President sent word that he would come. A large number of visitors had made their plans for three days only, and the Committee had grave fear that the President's address would be an anti-climax, instead of being what they had originally hoped. However, they made new plans for the fourth day. The President arrived on a special train at eleven o'clock, and was met by the bands and the dignitaries, and conducted to the tent, which was by no means full. The photographs show many empty chairs even on the platform. The President delivered his address, longer, to be sure, than that of Lincoln, but still very short, and went back to his train and left before noon. His speech began with the pronoun "I," and he used it eight times in less than as many minutes.

Theodore Roosevelt spoke at Gettysburg in the years 1904 and 1912, and each time on Memorial Day. At the time of his first appearance, he was immensely popular, and his visit added much to his Gettysburg popularity. The crowd was vast, and special trains were run from many cities. Five automobiles were there, the first ever seen in Gettysburg, frightening the horses that occupied the public roads from side to side, and raising questions as to whether this new and preposterous contraption had any future worth talking about. Roosevelt spoke that day to an eager crowd. Eight years later he came again, and was then in political disfavor. Only a half-dozen men shook hands with him when he arrived at the station; the crowd that heard him was small; the address was platitudinous, and the audience was cold at the outset and displeased at the close. All of which I learn from the Gettysburg *Times* and from people who were present. The second address was not reported in the press; but the first one was printed practically in full. I read it carefully, pencil in hand to count and add the uses of the first personal pronoun. The address was admirable and wholly impersonal. Theodore Roosevelt contradicted all my preconceived theories. Not once did he say "I."

Lincoln, probably, never had the slightest inclination to say "I" in his Gettysburg speech; few Presidents would have avoided it.

CHAPTER XX

"That Reminds Me of a Story"

If Abraham Lincoln were living now, and he were reading this book or participating in the discussion which it records, it is altogether probable that by this time or earlier a faint smile would be discovered giving its peculiar twitch to his lower lip, and he would say, "That reminds me of a story."

It reminds me of more than one story, illustrative of the extent and variety of the evidence that comes to us concerning the Gettysburg Address. In the next chapter we are to consider some of this evidence as we have it at first hand. We may now consider for a moment what would be our fate if we had only one account of the address from the pen of an honest and intelligent hearer of it, and what a bottomless abyss of misinformation we should be plunged into if we were to include in this volume all the testimony that has been given us at second hand. A single illustration will suffice.

Late in the year 1925 a newspaper discussion broke out, as such discussion does break out periodically, as to whether Lincoln's address at Gettysburg was original. Sir Hall Caine, the distinguished English novelist, with a zeal fully equal to his knowledge, leaped into the arena. He said that Lincoln had, indeed, used "some phrases which were taken from the common stock of immortal writing." He said that he himself, a few years previous, had found in the preface to Wycliff's translation of the English Bible the great phrase, "government of the people, by the people, for the

152

people." That was important information, for as far as I am aware, Sir Hall Caine is the sole and only man who has ever been able to find that phrase there. After some additional information concerning the literary character of the address, he proceeded to give what he declared was the correct history of Lincoln's preparation and delivery of it:

"My authority is, I think, the best possible, John Hay, who told me at his house in Washington the whole history of the speech, its origin and effect. John Hay, afterward Secretary of State, was Lincoln's private secretary at the time. He was alone with Lincoln the night before the speech, he went down alone with him to Gettysburg, and he sat one foot behind him while he was speaking.

"I was Hay's only guest at luncheon, and I told him I had spent the morning at the great Washington library, where the librarian had given me an account of the speech and its reception—how it had been spoken in a shrill, thin, ineffectual voice (which had been scarcely audible a dozen yards from the speaker) and had utterly failed in its delivery. Hay was indignant. 'So you, too, have heard that ridiculous story,' he said, and then, with a certain heat, he gave his own account of what happened.

"Hay's story, of which I have the clearest memory, was this: Lincoln was very silent all the previous evening after dinner, no one else being present. He walked to and fro in his room, apparently thinking deeply. He went to bed early, and when he came down to breakfast he looked unwell and said he had slept little. On the train he was silent for a considerable time, and then asked Hay for some writing-paper. On his knee he then wrote out his speech in full, exactly as it has come down to us. The impression left on Hay was that Lincoln was merely transcribing from memory the words he had composed during the night.

"When they reached the battle-field, Lincoln was nervous and apparently not well. Everett spoke eloquently, but very long. Then Lincoln rose, holding in his hand the papers he had written on the train. He did not read, but spoke every word in a clear, ringing, resonant, vibrating voice, which obviously passed over the crowd. His speech occupied only a few minutes in delivery. It was listened to with breathless attention, and when it came to an end there was at first no cheering, but an audible indrawing of deep breath as from an audience that had been profoundly moved. In the silence of the next moment Everett leapt to his feet again and said, as nearly as I can remember, this: 'We have just listened to a speech that will ring through the ages.' . . .

"May I say in conclusion that having read the great oration very many times, I am no longer sure that it is absolutely impeccable in point of style, but I still think that in nobility of spirit and majesty of phrase, it is unequaled by any modern utterance, and only to be matched by some of the most moving passages in the Hebrew prophets, outside the sublime Sayings of One whose words have, in my judgment, no parallel in human speech."

Now if we had no other testimony, we should be disposed to say, "John Hay was a man of unquestioned veracity, and Sir Hall Caine is a man of probity and of clear memory; this is reliable history." It makes us tremble to realize that most history is written on far less direct evidence. But John Hay did not go down alone with Lincoln to Gettysburg, and was not with him alone the night before the address, and very nearly everything else that Sir Hall Caine thought he clearly remembered is something that we know to have been untrue. John Hay had abundant opportunity to tell this story to others if it had been true, and

so far as we know he never told to any one a story that even
remotely resembled that which Sir Hall Caine thought he
remembered. John Hay certainly did not lie, and Sir Hall
Caine did not intend to falsify. But what a mess his story
makes! Of one thing we are instantly assured: the mistakes
are Hall Caine's; they can not be John Hay's. And that
reminds me of another story.

Allusion has already been made to the fact that,
as the fiftieth anniversary of the battle of Gettysburg
approached, the state of Pennsylvania made elaborate preparation for a notable commemoration of the event. It is
safe to say that no battle of the Civil War had any such
celebration as this one. For three successive days the
exercises continued, and on the fourth of July there was a
celebration of the nation's birthday which, though certainly
regarding its chief feature somewhat less impressive than
had been planned, was, after all, fitting as an intended climax. The real climax, however, occurred on the third day.
From the survivors of Pickett's Division, one hundred and
twenty old men had been assembled, and on that afternoon
they undertook to repeat their charge. They did not march
the entire distance; they were too old and the day was too
hot; but they lined up, facing the stone wall, and awaited
the order to charge. Behind the wall were one hundred and
eighty men who had been there once before. When the
hundred and twenty old men in gray had run or walked or
hobbled as best they could across the intervening space, and
approached the wall, the hundred and eighty rose up to
meet the attack. The old men in blue flung their arms
around the old men in gray and they sat down and drank
coffee together.

I think I could have seen the battle itself without tears;
but if I had been in Gettysburg on that day fifty years later,
I should have wanted to observe that charge unseen.

In elaborate and suitable fashion, Gettysburg commemorated the semi-centennial of the battle itself; but when the fiftieth anniversary of the Lincoln address drew near, only a local celebration was planned for its commemoration. There was a celebration, however, and for an account of it I am indebted to Ralph Parlette, editor of *The Lyceum* magazine. He tells it in humorous vein, but I have no doubt he tells it with substantial accuracy:

"In the autumn of 1913 I lectured at a teachers' institute in Gettysburg, and found that the bureau had left the next day open. This day was November 19, the anniversary day of Lincoln's Gettysburg speech. The late Ex-Governor Frank Hanly of Indianapolis was with me, he being slated to lecture that night in a town hard by. We conceived the idea of having the survivors who had heard Lincoln give the address, sit on the platform. We were able to muster four old men, and we put them in places of honor on the Gettysburg opera house stage. These old men went to sleep during Hanly's address, despite his enthusiasm. Then I as chairman, stated that we were honored to have with us a splendid citizen, who would now rise and tell us what he remembered of the great event. We had to wake him, and he tottered to his feet and said, 'Well, my friends, it was a rainy day, and I heard Mr. Lincoln speak in a loud voice, etc.' Great applause.

"Then I announced that the Lord had been kind in sparing another old veteran to this great day, and he would now rise and tell what he knew about it. This old veteran was properly roused and getting up said, 'Ladies and gentlemen, I remember that day well indeed. The sun shone clear and there wasn't a cloud in the sky, but Mr. Lincoln couldn't be heard, he spoke so low.'

"A titter went over the audience. Then we got the third

old man to rise, and he told a story entirely different. Now the crowd was laughing. And finally when the fourth citizen got up and contradicted all the others, the crowd roared, and the patriotic observance became almost a farce."

It is never safe to print a story like this without verifying it. Mr. Parlette is a truthful man, but truthful men seldom tell the truth. So I consulted the Gettysburg *Times* to see whether Mr. Parlette was really there, and whether Ex-Governor Hanly spoke, and whether four citizens of Gettysburg participated. The affair was reported, and very well reported, in the *Times,* at a length of over three columns. As seen by a Gettysburg editor, the Hanly address did not bulk so large as with Mr. Parlette. The report would appear to raise the question whether that address was not tacked on to a celebration already adequate and quite long enough. One could not wonder that the old men went to sleep. The four old men are named in the report, and much is said about them. Their divergence did not impress the editor as much as it did Mr. Parlette. They were very reputable citizens, and the names of two of them, with their narratives, appear in this book. But Mr. Parlette was there, just as he says, and did introduce Ex-Governor Hanly, just as he affirms, and whoever wishes to discover how well the very worthy old gentlemen agreed, can judge rather adequately from some of the pages that follow.

This little story is intended to illustrate the truth that we can not depend even on eye-witnesses to give us strictly accurate descriptions of their own experiences. And if reply be made to the effect that these four old men of Gettysburg were untrained to reflect and report their experiences, then I am reminded of another story, and that is one concerning a man of whom the same can not be said, for he was that

acute, scholarly, discriminating historian, Henry Cabot
Lodge. This story I quote from that interesting volume by
my friend, Dr. Charles Moore, on *Lincoln's Gettysburg Address and Second Inaugural*. Writing of the divergence of
testimony concerning the Gettysburg Address, Doctor
Moore says:

"A most significant case in point came into the experience of the writer. In 1921 I sent to that careful student
of history, Senator Henry Cabot Lodge, reproductions of
the first and second drafts of the Gettysburg Address. He
thought it curious that there should be such doubt about the
actual originals; for, he said, when Theodore Roosevelt was
inaugurated, on March 4, 1905, he, as a member of the
Senate Committee, was at the White House before the
President started for the Capitol. There he saw John Hay
give to President Roosevelt what the Senator understood,
and what he certainly was told, was the original rough draft
of the Gettysburg Address. He remembered that the President showed it to him with great delight. He accounted
for the fact that it was not among the Roosevelt papers
by stating that he felt certain Mrs. Roosevelt would keep it
among her personal possessions. The copy he saw, as he
recalled, was on slips of small note-paper size, written, he
would say, in pencil. Could testimony be more explicit or
circumstantial? Mrs. Roosevelt, on being appealed to, replied: 'Senator Lodge has a memory that I seem to
lack. Mr. Hay gave my husband a ring set with Lincoln's
hair, which is tucked away in my safe, and of which we
often spoke. Of the Gettysburg Address manuscript I
have not the slightest recollection.' Senator Lodge,
his memory being refreshed, said: 'Of course I remember the ring perfectly, but I must be wrong about
the Gettysburg Address, and that must be connected

with something else, because Mrs. Roosevelt would be sure
to be right about it, as she is about the ring.' "

Is it possible to find a more convincing case of fallibility
of a memory supposed to be disciplined to precision?

I quote this at length, because the next chapter is to
contain something like a reproduction, on a larger scale, of
that meeting in the Gettysburg opera-house. Whoever
reads that portion of this book will discover that a considerable number of truthful men, some of them men of special
training, have written their recollections of Gettysburg and
have contradicted one another at almost every point. I am
recording their reminiscences. They are valuable. None
of them are intentionally untruthful. I have profited by
the study of all of them. To write a book which attempts
to tell the Gettysburg story on the testimony of some one
man who was there would be a very simple and labor-sav-
ing way of writing history, but I have not chosen that
method. Neither have I been willing to hurl the reader into
the depths of a mass of discordant recollection. This testimony, after all, is not hopeless. Nor are we wholly shut
up in its consideration. When we compare it with other
evidence, the facts gradually emerge. What the facts are,
I have already stated, as I believe them; but if the reader
wishes to form opinions of his own, he will find material
in the next chapter. I have made no attempt to harmonize
it, and have not cared even to attempt an orderly arrangement.

The method I have pursued in this book has been that
of telling the story of Lincoln's speech at Gettysburg in
accordance with what I believe to be the facts. It appeared
to me better not to take the reader out into the tangled
jungle of conflicting recollection and confuse him with
irreconcilable testimony. It has been a task of years to

assemble the evidence and to gather the truth from it. That truth, as I regard it, has been told in the foregoing pages. But the reader has a right to know something of the evidence on which I have relied, and I am about to present it, not in full, for that would make a library instead of a volume, but in adequate variety. The reader may either satisfy himself that the author's conclusions are correct, or may form other opinions of his own.

CHAPTER XXI

SOME OF THOSE WHO HEARD IT

1. Senator Cornelius Cole

THE Honorable Cornelius Cole, who began his second century in 1923, and died at the age of one hundred and two, was said to have been at the time of his death the sole surviving member of the Thirty-seventh Congress. He was an alumnus of Wesleyan University of the class of 1847. In 1922 he returned to his alma mater, received an honorary degree, and at the commencement banquet spoke of what all who were present most wanted to hear, the Gettysburg Address. His speech was reported stenographically in the *Wesleyan Alumnus,* and is in part as follows:

"I realize that all persons connected with schools think more or less of the subject of literature, and it occurred to me this morning that I should make some remarks touching on a piece of literature that has called for great attention. I refer to the Gettysburg speech. And briefly I will say that late in the year 1863, perhaps a week or two before the first meeting of the Thirty-eighth Congress, the people of Pennsylvania engaged at Washington conceived the idea of creating a cemetery on the battleground of Gettysburg, in Pennsylvania, for the burial of the dead of that battle. The people engaged for the orator of the occasion Edward Everett, whose reputation as an orator at that time was very high. And they desired Mr. Lincoln also to attend the celebration, not as an orator, but that the people might see him and he see the people. They had some trouble in getting the consent of Mr. Lincoln to go up to Gettysburg, for the reason that the war was then in a very exciting state, and he could not well leave the Capitol to deliver an oration, for the military affairs engaged his whole time. However, he consented to go up; and I am quite sure that no member of his cabinet or any other member of his government went up with him. There were a few people in Washington, as visitors, who went up on that occasion, and I was one. I was not there as a visitor either, because, as a member of Congress, I was busy in making my preparations for the session that was soon to open.

"We arrived at Gettysburg late in the evening. There was no hotel in Gettysburg. Mr. Lincoln was assigned for the night to sleep with the mayor, or chief man, of Gettysburg. I and a few others were assigned for the night with a very wealthy person of the locality by the name of Featherstone, who afterwards figured in the affairs of the country in connection with Jay Cooke.

"The next morning we visited the battleground in carriages or such other way as was possible. Toward noon the population gathered where preparations had been made for the dedication of the cemetery. A large open platform, perhaps twenty or thirty feet in diameter, without any canopy, had been erected and some seats placed in front to accommodate the people. Soon all were seated, those who occupied the platform and those who were visitors. It was not a large attendance, as many might suppose. The people of Gettysburg perhaps were all present, but Gettysburg was a small town, and the people of the country came for the purpose, no doubt, of seeing the President.

"When all were seated, without any preparation in advance or ceremonies for the dedication, Mr. Everett arose and, with a little stand before him upon which was his speech, delivered his oration. It was quite long, but I observed, sitting by his side, that he paid no attention to his manuscript or speech on his platform whatever. He had learned it all by heart and went through it without any reference to his notes.

"When he took his seat, which he did without any applause, Mr. Lincoln arose and stepped forward to occupy the place where Mr. Everett had stood. It has been stated that Mr. Lincoln had prepared his speech in writing, that he had done so on the way from Washington. There is no foundation for a statement of that kind. Mr. Lincoln probably made not a word or note in preparation for that address. I have no doubt whatever that it was entirely extempore and called forth by the circumstances of the occasion. And I think if any of you scholars will analyze it, you will come to the conclusion that that must have been the case. Mr. Lincoln was not expected to be the orator of the day. He opened his speech by saying, 'Four score and seven years ago our fathers brought forth upon this continent,' and so on through, speaking of the war and of those that had fallen, and ending with the hope that this government 'of the people, by the people, for the people' might never perish.

"Then he took his seat very suddenly. It was such a disappointment to everybody that there was no applause of any kind."

2. Governor William Dennison

Honorable Isaac N. Arnold, for many years a personal friend of Lincoln, the most staunch and loyal of all his supporters throughout Lincoln's term of office, and the administrator of Lincoln's estate after his death, was not per-

sonally present at Gettysburg, but wrote on the authority
of Governor Dennison and other eye-witnesses:

"Here, on the 19th of November, with solemn, touching, and most impressive ceremonies, this ground was consecrated to its pious purpose. The President, his Cabinet,
and officials of the state of Pennsylvania, governors of
states, foreign ministers, officers of the army and navy,
soldiers and citizens, gathered in great numbers to witness
the proceedings. Edward Everett, late Secretary of State,
and Senator from Massachusetts, an orator and scholar
whose renown had extended over the world, was selected to
pronounce the oration. He was a polished and graceful
speaker, and worthy of the theme and the occasion. President Lincoln, while in the cars on his way from the White
House to the battle-field, was notified that he would be expected to make some remarks also. Asking for some paper,
a rough sheet of foolscap was handed to him, and, retiring
to a seat by himself, with a pencil, he wrote the address
which has become so celebrated; an address which for
appropriateness and eloquence, for pathos and beauty, for
sublimity in sentiment and expression, has hardly its equal
in English or American literature. Everett's oration was a
polished specimen of consummate oratorical skill. It was
memorized, and recited without referring to a note. It was
perhaps too artistic; so much so, that the audience sometimes during its delivery forgot the heroic dead to admire
the skill of the speaker before them. When at length the
New England orator closed, and the cheers in his honor had
subsided, an earnest call for Lincoln was heard through the
vast crowd in attendance. Slowly, and very deliberately,
the tall, homely form of the President rose; simple, rude,
his careworn face now lighted and glowing with intense
feeling. All unconscious of himself, absorbed with recollec-

Four score and seven years ago our fathers brought forth, on this continent, a new nation, conceived in Liberty, and dedicated to the proposition that all men are created equal.

Now we are engaged in a great civil war, testing whether that nation, or any nation so conceived, and so dedicated, can long endure. We are met on a great battle-field of that war. We have come to dedicate a portion of that field, as a final resting-place for those who here gave their lives, that that nation might live. It is altogether fitting and proper that we should do this.

But, in a larger sense, we can not dedicate— we can not consecrate— we can not hallow— this ground. The brave men, living and dead, who struggled here, have consecrated it far above our poor power to add or detract. The world will little note, nor long remember what we say here, but it can never forget what they did here. It is for us the living, rather, to be dedicated here to the unfinished work which they who fought here have thus far so nobly advanced. It is rather for us to be here dedicated to the great task remaining be-

The Gettysburg Address as Lincoln wrote it at the request of Hon. George Bancroft

fore us — that from these honored dead we take increased devotion to that cause for which they here gave
the last full measure of devotion — that we here highly resolve that these dead shall not have died in
vain — that this nation, under God, shall have
a new birth of freedom — and that government
of the people, by the people, for the people, shall
not perish from the earth.

Executive Mansion,
Washington, Feb. 29, 1864.

Hon. George Bancroft
My dear Sir.

Herewith is the copy
of the manuscript which you did
me the honor to request.

Yours truly
A. Lincoln.

tions of the heroic dead, he adjusted his spectacles, and read with most profound feeling the address.

"Before the first sentence was completed, a thrill of feeling, like an electric shock, pervaded the crowd. That mysterious influence called magnetism, which sometimes so affects a popular assembly, spread to every heart. The vast audience was instantly hushed, and hung upon his every word and syllable. When he uttered the sentence: 'the world will little *note* nor long remember what we *say,* here, but it can never forget what they *did* here,' every one felt that it was not the 'honored dead' only, but the living actor and speaker, that the world for all time to come would note and remember, and that he, the speaker, in the thrilling words he was uttering, was linking his name forever with the glory of the dead. He seemed so absorbed in honoring 'the heroic sacrifices' of the soldiers, as utterly to forget himself, but all his hearers realized that the great actor in the drama stood before them, and that the words he was speaking would live as long as the language; that they were words which would be recalled in all future ages, among all peoples; as often as men should be called upon to die for liberty and country.

"Thus were the immortal deeds of the dead commemorated in immortal words. There have been four instances in history in which great deeds have been celebrated in words as immortal as themselves; the well-known epitaph upon the Spartans who perished at Thermopylæ, the words of Demosthenes on those who fell at Marathon, the speech of Webster in memory of those who died at Bunker Hill, and these words of Lincoln in honor of those who laid down their lives on the field of Gettysburg.

"As he closed, and the tears, and sobs, and cheers which expressed the emotions of the people subsided, he turned to Everett, and grasping his hand, said: 'I congratulate you on your success.' The orator gracefully replied: 'Ah, Mr. President, how gladly would I exchange all my hundred pages to have been the author of your twenty lines.' ''

3. Honorable Horatio King

Honorable Horatio King, at one time Postmaster-General of the United States, was not present at Gettysburg, but the chapter on this subject in his book *Turning on the Light,* is important because he early interviewed a number of men who were there, and made careful notes of what they told him. Omitting some of his quotations, because they are actual, or virtual duplicates of those of men present whom we are preferring to quote in their own words, this is his account of the event:

"There have been so many conflicting statements about President Lincoln's Gettysburg speech that I have taken pains to bring some of them together with a view to see if there is any way to get at the truth. In the first place, as to the manner of its writing and delivery.

"The reporter of the New York *Times,* as quoted by the Springfield *Republican,* says Mr. Lincoln spoke from manuscript, referring to it as often as once for each sentence; that he spoke in a loud voice and was loudly applauded. He says that when the President had finished, it is related that Mr. Everett, the orator of the day, who had spoken before him, grasped Mr. Lincoln's hand warmly and said, in substance, 'What I have said here will be forgotten, but your words will live.'

"Mr. John Russell Young, who, as reporter for the Philadelphia *Press,* was also present, states that Mr. Lincoln 'took the single sheet of foolscap, held it almost to his nose, and, in his high tenor voice, without the least attempt

for effect, delivered that most extraordinary address.
There were four or five thousand people present. Very
few heard what Mr. Lincoln said, and it is a curious thing
that his remarkable words should have made no particular
impression at the time.'

"Now listen to what Andrew G. Curtin, the distinguished war Governor and statesman of Pennsylvania, says.
Remembering to have heard him relate the story of the
writing and delivery of Mr. Lincoln's extraordinary address,
which now 'belongs to the classics of literature'—it was in
May, 1885, while riding with him and others over the
battle-field, and when he pointed out to me the house of
Mr. Wills, in the village, where, he says, he saw Mr. Lincoln engaged in writing it—I called on him at his hotel in
this city a few days ago, and, with pencil in hand to make
sure of his exact words, asked him to repeat the account.
He said:

"'I saw Mr. Lincoln writing his address in Mr. (now
Judge) Wills' house, on a long yellow envelope. He may
have written some of it before. He said, "I will go and
show it to Seward," who stopped at another house, which
he did, and then returned and copied his speech on a foolscap sheet. The people outside were calling now on Mr.
Lincoln for a speech, and he got me to go and speak for
him. Mr. Lincoln rode on horseback to the field, where a
temporary stand had been erected. After the oration of
Mr. Everett and the singing of a dirge by the Baltimore
Glee Club, Mr. Lincoln proceeded to speak. He rose and
presented himself in a most dignified manner, becoming a
President of the United States. He pronounced that
speech in a voice that all the multitude heard. The crowd
was hushed into silence because the President stood before
them. But at intervals there were roars of applause. My
God! it was so impressive! It was the common remark of

everybody. Such a speech, as they said it was! Everett and all went and congratulated the President, shaking him by the hand.'

"Governor Curtin, on the former as well as on the present occasion, expressed extreme regret that he had not secured that envelope on which he most positively declares he saw Mr. Lincoln writing his address, as above described.

"Finally, I am happy to be able to add one more item, not less interesting, touching this controverted subject. I have the statement from General Joseph Holt direct, that a day or two after Mr. Lincoln's return from Gettysburg, while signing some papers which he (General H.), as Judge-Advocate-General, had brought for his signature, the President looked up with lively satisfaction and remarked, 'I have just received a letter from Mr. Everett, in which he says that I had said more in my little speech than he had said in his whole oration.'

"Having presented the above rather conflicting testimony, [concludes Mr. King] I believe I will submit the case 'to the jury'—my readers—without either 'summing up' or 'argument,' premising, however, that I am inclined to stand by the grand old war Governor."

4. Honorable Benjamin B. French

We have an account of the service from the pen of the Honorable Benjamin Brown French. He became a somewhat noted interpreter of the event, and on one occasion, February 19, 1869, he went to Gettysburg to deliver an address on the subject before the Theological Seminary at Gettysburg. A letter and poem which grew out of this visit, now constitute a rare Lincoln item. Mr. French kept a diary, which, in 1904, was edited, and "a few copies" were "printed for private circulation only" by his grandson, Amos Tuck French.

This account may now be summarized:

"Gettysburg, Nov. 22. Sun. Morning.

". . . Mr. Everett was listened to with breathless silence by all that immense crowd, and he had his audience in tears many times during his masterly effort."

It should be remarked that Mr. French, as author of the hymn, had a place of honor on the platform, and witnessed the close attention and deep sympathy of those close at hand, while others, nearer the outskirts of the crowd, thought that the audience as a whole grew very weary, and that most of them scattered before the end of the two hours.

Mr. French then wrote of the singing of his own composition, and proceeded: "I was never so much flattered at any production of my own."

He then quoted the words of his hymn, and continued: "As soon as the hymn was sung, Marshal Lamon introduced the President of the United States, who in a few brief words dedicated the cemetery."

This is the hymn that Mr. French had written and which he quoted in his account of the occasion.

" 'Tis holy ground—
This spot, where, in their graves,
We place our country's braves,
Who fell in Freedom's holy cause,
Fighting for liberties and laws;
    Let tears abound.

"Here let them rest;
'And summer's heat and winter's cold

Shall glow and freeze above this mould—
A thousand years shall pass away—
A nation still shall mourn this clay,
 Which now is blest.

"Here, where they fell,
Oft shall the widow's tear be shed,
Oft shall fond parents mourn their dead;
The orphan here shall kneel and weep,
And maidens, where their lovers sleep,
 Their woes shall tell.

"Great God in Heaven!
Shall all this sacred blood be shed?
Shall we thus mourn our glorious dead?
Oh, shall the end be wrath and woe,
The knell of Freedom's overthrow,
 A country riven?

"It will not be!
We trust, O God! thy gracious power
To aid us in our darkest hour.
This be our prayer—'O Father! save
A people's freedom from its grave.
 All praise to Thee!' "

He then quoted the address of the President, and went
on:

"Abraham Lincoln is the idol of the American people
at this moment. Any one who saw and heard the hurricane
of applause that met his every word at Gettysburg would
know that he lived in every heart. It was no cold shadow
of a kind reception. It was a tumultuous outpouring from
true and loving hearts at the sight of a man whom everyone

knew to be honest and sincere in every act of his life and every pulsation of his heart. It was the spontaneous outburst of heartfelt confidence in *their own President.*"

5. *Professor John W. Draper*

Professor Draper in his *History of the American Civil War,* one of the most scholarly of treatises on that subject, states that Lincoln, being introduced at Gettysburg, rose, and

"He unpremeditatedly and solemnly said, 'It is intimated to me that this assemblage expects me to say something on this occasion.'"

6. *Honorable Edward McPherson*

Honorable Edward McPherson, for many years Clerk of the House of Representatives in Washington, and author of an important documentary *History of the Civil War,* a man who had long and careful training in matters of public address, and who was in close contact with most if not all of the participants in the event, was, besides all this, a resident of Gettysburg. He said that Lincoln, having retired for the night, sent for Mr. Wills, and

"He inquired the order of exercises for the next day and began to put in writing what he called some stray thoughts to utter on the morrow.

"Mr. Wills believed that this was the first writing of the address, and that Lincoln later in the evening went over to the near-by house where Secretary Seward lodged, read the address to him, returned and made some corrections and used the same manuscript next day."

7. *Governor Andrew G. Curtin*

In Mowry's *History of the United States for Schools* published in 1896, it is said:

"There is conclusive evidence that the words of the address were not written out until the Presidential party arrived on the ground. . . . The following account of how the address was written was received directly from ex-Governor Curtin, of Pennsylvania, who was present on the occasion and knew whereof he affirmed. Governor Curtin said that after the arrival of the party from Washington, while the President and his Cabinet, Edward Everett, the orator of the day, Governor Curtin, and others were sitting in the parlor of the hotel, the President remarked that he understood that the committee expected him to say something. He would, therefore, if they would excuse him, retire to the next room and see if he could write out something. He was absent some time, and upon returning to the company had in his hand a large-sized yellow envelope. The President sat down, and remarked that he had written something, and with their permission would like to read it to them, and invited them to criticize it. After reading what he had written upon the envelope, he asked for any suggestions they might make; Secretary Seward volunteered one or two comments, which Mr. Lincoln accepted and incorporated. Then he said, 'Now, gentlemen, if you will excuse me again, I will copy this off,' and returning again made a fresh copy to read from."

I knew Mr. Mowry, and he was a reliable man. He recited this story to me, and recorded it in his book, as he had heard it from Governor Curtin, a trustworthy man and a very capable Governor.

8. Ben Perley Poore

Ben Perley Poore, one of the most astute of all Washington correspondents of his time, said in his *Reminiscences of Lincoln* of his remarks at Gettysburg that they "were written in the car on the way from Washington to the battlefield, upon a piece of pasteboard held on his knee."

9. General James B. Fry

General James B. Fry, who was in the car with Lincoln, says: "I have no recollection of seeing him writing or even reading his speech during the journey; in fact there was hardly any opportunity for him to read or write."

10. General Julius H. Stahl

General Stahl, who was in charge of the escort, said:

"I escorted President Lincoln from Washington to Gettysburg, and was with him in the same car when he wrote something on his knees, which I fully believe was the famous address which he delivered at the battle-field. I was near him when he delivered that world-wide and celebrated dedication address. I well remember that Lincoln seemed to be impressed with the solemnity of the occasion, and delivered the oration in accord with his well-known benevolent nature, in a calm, earnest, dignified manner; and that the same was received and listened to by all by-standers with reverence due to the occasion. . . . I do not remember that it was received with plaudit, but I know that it was received with the solemnity due to the occasion."

11. Andrew Carnegie

Among those who believed that Lincoln wrote the Gettysburg Address on the train, is said to have been Andrew Carnegie. George S. Hellman, in his *Lanes of*

Memory, relates that Carnegie told Herbert Spencer and Charles M. Schwab, and probably others, that he was Secretary to the President of the Baltimore and Ohio Railroad, and accompanied his chief on the train as he went with Lincoln from Baltimore to Gettysburg. Carnegie affirmed, as this narrative declares, that it was he who lent Lincoln the pencil with which he wrote whatever he did write on the way to Gettysburg.

12. *Adjutant Robert Miller*

The Eaton, Ohio, *Register* of November 30, 1863, contained this account of the dedication, by Adjutant Robert Miller, who served in an Ohio regiment and, as a member of the Ohio Legislature, attended the dedication:

"The tall form of the President appeared on the stand and never before have I seen a crowd so vast and restless, after standing so long, so soon stilled and quieted. Hats were removed and all stood motionless to catch the first words he should utter, and as he slowly, clearly, and without the least sign of embarrassment read and spoke for ten minutes you could not mistake the feeling and sentiment of the vast multitude before him. I am convinced that the speech of the President has fully confirmed and I think will confirm all loyal men and women in the belief that Abraham Lincoln, though he may have made mistakes, is the right man in the right place."

13. *Reverend Julius B. Remensnyder*

Practically all the students in the theological seminary at Gettysburg heard Lincoln, and as they were graduated into the ministry and had frequent occasion to relate their experiences, they became among the most frequently quoted of witnesses, and in some respects among the most reliable. The Reverend Dr. Julius B. Remensnyder, one of the most noted of Lutheran ministers in the United States, has told on various occasions of his impressions. He, in common with many other students, formed a very unfavorable opinion of the President on the night of his arrival, for they were present at the serenade, and thought him abrupt and rude in the manner of his refusal to speak. This impression was deepened next day as they witnessed his ungainly appearance on a horse too small, and his attitude as he sat in the large rocking-chair on the platform while Mr. Everett was speaking. But the young student, Remensnyder, was able to show in later years the entry he made in his diary that night, saying "It was as fine a speech as I ever heard."

Doctor Remensnyder's account of the event is thus recorded:

"President Lincoln arrived the evening before. We learned that he was quartered at the house of Colonel Wills, situated on the public square, so we surrounded the house and noisily clamored for him. At last the President appeared on the balcony, remarking that as his words at such a time would be widely reported he would defer what he had to say to the morrow's address.

"November 19th dawned bright and clear—a perfect day for the ceremonial. An imposing pageant of generals, governors, soldiers and officials was formed to proceed to the cemetery, located on a gentle hill, just outside the town. At its head rode the President, mounted on so small a horse that his long limbs nearly touched the ground. A platform, perhaps sixty feet square, had been built for the distinguished guests. A rudely constructed rocking chair was provided for the President. The crowd kept swelling, until fully twenty thousand people pressed about the platform. Another student and I had taken the precaution to select a favored spot for seeing and hearing.

"Mr. Everett fully rose to the occasion. His speech, which was two hours long, was dignified in manner, eloquent and impassioned in delivery, and was concluded amid great and general applause.

"It was then announced that President Lincoln would dedicate the cemetery. All eyes at once centered upon him. For it was felt that he was the soul of the great national struggle. He arose calmly, took out his paper and, holding it in both hands, proceeded to read it. An intense silence gripped the vast gathering. Every sentence phrased some vital feature of the conflict. It seemed to rise higher and higher, until it reached the eloquent climax, which he pronounced with especial emphasis, 'that we here highly resolve that these dead shall not have died in vain; that this nation, under God, shall have a new birth of freedom, and that government of the people, by the people, for the people, shall not perish from the earth.' The address was so brief, and the audience was held by such a spell, that for an instant profound stillness reigned. Then arose an outburst of general applause.

"Mr. Everett was the first to speak to the President, 'I would congratulate myself,' he said, 'if I thought I said as much in two hours as you have said in two minutes. Your speech will be remembered long after mine is forgotten.' I at once asked my fellow student, who was from the South, what he thought of it? 'Mighty good, for Father Abe,' he replied.

"Controversy has arisen as to President Lincoln's reading the address or merely holding it in his hand. I affirm positively that he held it and apparently read every word of it. And my statement is confirmed by a correspondent charged by a leading paper to photograph the President while delivering the address, who writes me that he found it impossible, for all the while the reader held the paper so that it concealed his face."

14. *Professor Philip H. Bikle*

Professor Philip H. Bikle said of it:

"Few can appreciate what an imposing occasion it was— one of the largest gatherings of men since the battle, and the first one honored by the President of the United States and members of his cabinet. Not only were these high civil officials present but a great many of high military rank. Indeed, the military feature was the most conspicuous, and the large procession and most of the other events were under military direction. Civic and fraternal organizations as well as military were given a place in the procession, but all were under the orders of a marshal who was a soldier of high rank.

"The way I got into that procession was because the students of college were given a place, and I was a student. We were assigned the inconspicuous position of tail-enders, and much to our regret, as many of us wanted to hear the speeches and we thought we should find ourselves on the outskirts of the crowd when we reached the cemetery. But we obeyed orders and all turned out well. According to instructions we assembled on York street in front of the Gettysburg National Bank and Mr. McCreary's residence. This was almost directly opposite the Wills building where Mr. Lincoln and most of his party were being entertained by Judge Wills. It gave us a most excellent opportunity to see the President and the distinguished men with him as they came out and mounted their horses to take the head of the procession when the order should come to do so. Fortunately the order did not come for twenty minutes or more after they had mounted, and we young men could not have had a better place for a good look at them. This was some compensation for being tail-enders, but better was yet to come. Many a regret was expressed, as we passed over Baltimore Hill and saw the thousands ahead of us, that we surely would miss the speeches. But who can tell our surprise when, on reaching the cemetery, we found that the column had divided and the tail-enders were allowed to march through and halt directly in front of the large platform built for the speakers and other dignitaries of that occasion? What a piece of luck this was, but, oh, what a jam it was too. I have never been so wedged in a crowd in my life as I was then, but I was determined to see it through.

"Mr. Everett was down for the principal speech and he gave a very long one. It had all the fine finish you might expect from such a polished rhetorician and orator, but on the whole it was disappointing as it was given mainly to the movements of the two armies that fought the battle of Gettysburg. But the crowd held together remarkably well. When Mr. Lincoln rose to speak the stillness was very noticeable. It was the tall, gaunt figure of a man that might be called somewhat imposing but certainly not attractive. But he was the head of the nation and reverenced. With a hand on each side of his manuscript the sheets of which were of typewriter size, he spoke in a most deliberate manner, and with such a forceful and articulate expression that he could be heard by all of that immense throng. It is seldom we have heard any one whose voice carried so well. There was no gesture except with both hands up and down, grasping the manuscript which he did not seem to need, as he looked at it so seldom. In this way he delivered the whole speech. I do not remember that there was any applause, but I do remember that there was surprise that his speech was so short. What the crowd thought of its merits I do not know, but I do know what I thought. On coming away I said to a classmate, 'Well, Mr. Lincoln's speech was simple, appropriate, and right to the point, but I don't think there was anything remarkable about it.' That was the opinion of a wise sophomore. Edward Everett's opinion was different. I think he would have said that its simplicity, appropriateness and pointedness are among the features that make it remarkable. The sophomore now sees it in its true light and will always rejoice that it was his privilege to hear it."

15. Professor H. C. Holloway

Professor H. C. Holloway thus gives his reminiscences:

"What I have to say on 'Lincoln at Gettysburg,' I give from personal observation. I was present and heard the immortal speech made by the immortal Lincoln on that momentous occasion. The now priceless journal I kept in those days is here under my eyes. It tells its own true and correct story. What I saw and heard that day went on record that evening.

"Extensive preparations had been made for this national event. The expectations were great. The fact that the President and his cabinet would grace the occasion was quite sufficient to create the liveliest interest. The distinguished party arrived in Gettysburg the evening before. They immediately proceeded to the residence of Hon. David Wills, who entertained Mr. Lincoln.

"In the meantime a great crowd had gathered in front of the Wills' mansion, and vigorously called for the Presi-

dent. Secretary Seward, of the cabinet, and Colonel Forney, of Philadelphia, responded in short speeches. But this
did not satisfy the multitudes. Nothing would do, the
President must come forth. He did, but made only a few
remarks, thanking the people for their cordial welcome, and
with a hearty good-night, disappeared. This part of the
evening was followed by a reception at the house of Mr.
Wills.

"The morning of the next day was beautiful. The sky
was cloudless, and the sun shone out in glorious splendor.
It was a great day in Gettysburg. The procession formed
in the square of the town. It was estimated that from
15,000 to 18,000 people were present. Military and civic
organizations from many parts of the nation participated.
It was a truly national occasion. The Marine Band of
Washington, D. C., was the leading organization in the way
of music. The President had about him the members of
his cabinet. Many other distinguished men of national
fame and reputation were present. The noted, brilliant
war governor of Pennsylvania, Andrew G. Curtin; Governors Tod, Dennison and Brough, of Ohio; Major Generals
Schenk, Couch and Stahl; also Brigadier Generals Buford,
Gibbon and others.

"In those days it was customary for dignitaries, on
special occasions, to ride on horse back. The committee
had provided a horse of fine style for the President. Possibly this horse was a bit below the average in height. After
he had mounted the animal, the difference was more perceptible, for Mr. Lincoln's feet were near the ground. The
spectacle was next to the humorous, and no one seemed more
conscious of it than himself. For all that, measuring six
feet and four inches in height, garbed in a long Prince
Albert coat, his head crowned with a full one-story silk hat,
the President towered above all his associates.

"The vast column, as it moved toward its destination, was impressive and beautiful. An air of solemnity seemed to possess the multitudes. It was a veritable funeral procession.

"After reaching the grounds, and the opening services, consisting of music and prayer, the distinguished orator of the day, Hon. Edward Everett, was introduced by Governor Andrew G. Curtin, of Pennsylvania. The oration of Mr. Everett was great, perfectly adapted to the occasion, and exactly what such an oration should be. At its close there was befitting music. Then Governor Curtin presented President Lincoln as only to accept in a few formal words, the cemetery grounds on behalf of the nation. I was not far from the speaker's stand. I easily heard and saw the movements of the distinguished speaker. His clear ringing voice carried his words all over that vast assembly. As the President began to speak I instinctively felt that the occasion was taking on a new grandeur, as of a great moment in history, and then there followed, in slow, clear and most impressive far-reaching utterance the words with which the whole world has long since been familiar.

"I am well aware that a difference of opinion has been expressed in regard to the reception by the people on the occasion of Mr. Lincoln's immortal speech. One writer in his little book entitled, 'The Perfect Tribute,' which purported to give the story of Lincoln's Gettysburg speech, speaks of how the President for weeks was under a cloud of remorse over his address, believing it had been a failure, etc. This is totally at variance with the facts in the case as we saw them. It is an unnatural interpretation of the occasion and does not comport with what actually occurred. The address was received with remarkable enthusiasm and in a manner becoming the great occasion.

"There was one disappointing feature about it—its

marked brevity. The speaker had, as we thought, but barely commenced when he stopped. The clear, ringing voice ceased before we were ready for it. There was a pause, between the close of the address and the applause because the people expected more; but when it was apparent that the address was really concluded, the applause was most hearty, rising like the sound of many waters.

"Among the numerous personal congratulations of the distinguished men present were the prophetic words of Hon. Edward Everett. He said: 'Mr. President, your speech will be remembered long after mine is forgotten.' The next day Mr. Everett wrote Mr. Lincoln a letter in which he expressed his great admiration for the address, and said: 'I should be glad if I could flatter myself that I came as near to the central idea of the occasion in my two hours as you did in two minutes.' In great earnestness, said Hon. Mr. MacVeagh to Mr. Lincoln, 'You have made an immortal address.' To whom the President replied quickly: 'Oh, you must not say that. You must not be extravagant about it.'

"Indeed, so great was that speech that no one at the time comprehended it fully. No eulogistic utterances in regard to it, can do it justice. As the ages go by it will lose none of its luster. We had heard very much more that day than we dreamed of."

16. Professor Henry E. Jacobs

Professor Henry Eyster Jacobs, who was a student in the Lutheran Seminary at the time of the battle, and who heard the address, has thus recorded his recollections:

"As Mr. Everett was closing his oration, Mr. Lincoln, I thought, was showing some of that nervousness which, according to Cicero, characterizes all successful oratory. His mind evidently was not on what Mr. Everett was saying, but on his own speech. He drew from his pocket a metallic spectacle case and adjusted a pair of steel glasses near the tip of his nose. Then, reaching into the side pocket of his coat, he produced a crumpled sheet of paper, which he first carefully smoothed and then read for a few minutes. By this time Mr. Everett had reached his final periods:

" 'Surely I would do no injustice to the other noble achievements of the war, which have reflected such honor on both arms of the service and have entitled the armies and navy of the United States, their officers and men, to the warmest thanks and the richest rewards which a grateful people can pay. But they, I am sure, will join me in saying, as we bid farewell to the dust of these martyr-heroes, that wheresoever throughout the civilized world the accounts of this great warfare are read, and down to the latest period of recorded time, in the glorious annals of our common country, there will be no brighter page than that which relates The Battles of Gettysburg.'

"Mr. Lincoln's notes had been placed again in his pocket, but his spectacles remained in position. A dirge was then sung. Every eye and ear was strained as the President arose, a majestic figure, in all the stateliness of his office and with the solemnity which befitted the occasion, not to deliver an oration but to formally dedicate the grounds. It was a sad hour. Any tumultuous wave of applause would have been out of place. The entire bearing of Mr. Lincoln showed how deeply he realized the seriousness of the act. It grieved him that there were many thousands who regarded him as personally responsible for the deaths which the exercises of the day called to mind. At no time more than when he stood before the newly-made graves of Gettysburg did the injustice of this charge so oppress him.

His sole effort, therefore, was to convince the world of the overwhelming importance of the principle for which the war was waged and the heroes of the battle had fallen and his own life was being spent.

"The deep feeling of the speaker, combined with masterful self-control and firmly set purpose, made a profound impression. There was something so unusual in the tones of his voice and in his mode of address, that long before those present were ready to weigh his words he had finished. His remarks were limited to nine sentences. The suddenness with which he ended was almost startling. The first few lines of the address were spoken without notes. Then gradually drawing them from his pocket, he held in both hands the sheet on which they were written, making emphatic gestures, not with his hands, which were preoccupied, but by bowing from side to side with his body. All told there were only two hundred and fifty words spoken, and just two minutes' time were occupied in their delivery. But rarely has the same amount of thought and argument been compressed within the same compass."

17. Honorable Wayne MacVeagh

One of the most competent of those who heard Mr. Lincoln and left a record of his impressions was Honorable Wayne MacVeagh, later Attorney General of the United States, who thus wrote:

"As he came forward he seemed to me, and I was sitting near to him, visibly to dominate the scene, and while over his plain and rugged countenance appeared to settle a great melancholy, it was somehow lightened by a great hope. As he began to speak I instinctively felt that the occasion was taking on a new grandeur, as of a great moment in history;

and then there followed, in a slow and very impressive and far-reaching utterance, the words with which the whole world has long been familiar,* As each word was spoken it appeared to me so clearly fraught with a message not only for us of his day, but for the untold generations of men, that before he concluded I found myself possessed of a reverential awe for its complete justification of the great war he was conducting, as if conducted, as in truth it was, in the interest of mankind. Surely at that moment he justified the inspired portraiture of Lowell in the 'Commemoration Ode.' "

18. Major A. H. Nickerson

One of the best and most interesting articles on the Gettysburg Address was published, thirty years later, written by Major A. H. Nickerson, of the Eighth Ohio. In *Scribner's Magazine,* for July, 1893, he told of his two visits to Gettysburg, in July and November, 1863. He was desperately and, as he then thought, fatally wounded in the battle, but defied all prognosis and recovered in time to attend the dedication services. He had seen Lincoln once or twice before and his narrative is of great interest:

"When Mr. Lincoln arose in obedience to the announcement that the President would now pronounce the dedication, everyone felt sorry for him. To say that Mr. Lincoln arose can only be appreciated by those who have been near him when he got up to speak; but he never before seemed to me to be so tall as he did on this occasion. He appeared to continue to arise, as it were, until, when he had finally stood up, I thought he was the tallest and most awkward man I had ever seen.

---

*The foregoing sentence may be compared with one in the account by Professor Holloway.

"There has been considerable difference of opinion among those who were present as to whether he used notes of this, undoubtedly the greatest speech of his life. My own impressions, which, whether correct or not, were received then and have never been changed by anything I have seen or heard on the subject. I think he had a card or a slip of paper the size of a visiting card in his hand. He did not, however, look at it, or refer to it in any way.

"Others, too, have differed as to the immediate effects of the President's remarks. I give the impressions received at the time, which were also identical with those of all with whom I spoke. I thought then, and still think, it was the shortest, grandest speech to which I had ever listened. . . . My own emotions may perhaps be imagined when it is remembered that he was facing the spot where only a short time before we had our death grapple with Pickett's men, and he stood almost immediately over the place where I had lain and seen my comrades torn in fragments by the enemy's cannon-balls—think, then, if you please, how these words fell on my ears.

[The major then quoted a portion of the address, and added:]

"If at that moment the Supreme Being had appeared to me with an offer to undo my past life, give back to me a sound body free from the remembrance even of sufferings past and those that must necessarily embitter all the years to come, I should have indignantly spurned the offer, such was the effect upon me of this immortal dedication."

19. General James Grant Wilson

"It was a cloudless and perfect autumn day, and thousands from far and near were assembled on the forever famous battlefield to listen to the oration of New England's

Four score and seven years ago our fathers brought forth upon this continent, a new nation, conceived in Liberty, and dedicated to the proposition that all men are created equal.

Now we are engaged in a great civil war, testing whether that nation, or any nation so conceived, and so dedicated, can long endure. We are met on a great battle-field of that war. We have come to dedicate a portion of that field, as a final resting place for those who here gave their lives, that that nation might live. It is altogether fitting and proper that we should do this.

But, in a larger sense, we can not dedicate— we can not consecrate— we can not hallow— this ground. The brave men, living and dead, who struggled here, have consecrated it, far above our poor power to add or detract. The world will little note, nor long remember, what we say here, but it can never forget what they did here. It is for us, the living, rather, to be dedicated here to the unfinished work which they who fought here, have, thus far, so nobly advanced. It is rather for us to be here dedicated to the great task remaining before us— that from these honored dead we take increased devotion to that cause for which they here gave the last full measure of devotion— that we here highly resolve that these dead shall not have died in vain— that this nation, under God, shall have a new birth of freedom— and that, government of the people, by the people, for the people, shall not perish from the earth.

The Keyes copy of the Gettysburg Address as Lincoln wrote it to be sold with the manuscript of Edward Everett's Address at the New York Sanitary Fair

most distinguished and classic living orator. Delivered with his accustomed grace, Edward Everett's long address was smooth and cold, lacking a single stirring thought, vivid picture or patriotic appeal.

"Then followed, at a few minutes before two o'clock, the President's short and simple speech, so felicitous and so perfect. Not a sound broke the solemn stillness. The immense audience that was within the sound of his strong tenor and far-reaching voice listened almost breathlessly during its delivery, which occupied precisely 135 seconds. While holding his manuscript of two sheets in his left hand, Lincoln made no use of it. As on the occasion of the President's second inaugural address, in March, 1865, there was a loud outburst of applause at its close, but it may be questioned if, either at Gettysburg or the nation's capital, these brief and perfect examples of English oratory were fully appreciated. They were the crowning efforts of his career as a public speaker."

20. *Major William H. Lambert*

Major William H. Lambert, in an able essay on the Gettysburg Address, quotes Samuel P. Bates, whose *History of the Battle of Gettysburg* says:

"Its delivery was more solemn and impressive than is possible to conceive from its perusal."

From this same volume he quotes Major Harry T. Lee, who had fought in the battle and was present at the address, who said that "The people listened with marked attention throughout the two hours that Mr. Everett spoke . . . but that when Mr. Lincoln came forward and, with a voice burdened with emotion, uttered these sublime

words, 'The brave men, living and dead, who struggled
here,' the bosoms of that vast audience were lifted as a
great wave of the sea, and there was not a dry eye."

21. *Honorable Joseph A. Gouldon*

On February 12, 1915, Honorable Joseph A. Gouldon,
of New York, said in the national House of Representatives
in Washington:

"It was my good fortune to be present and hear the address from its author's lips. . . . The day was so impressive in itself, and after events so fixed in my mind that its
central facts are still as clear and vivid as though it were
yesterday. When the President came forward, after the
finished oration of Mr. Everett, he looked tired and seemed
nervous. Hearty applause greeted him as he stepped forward to the front of the platform. With his right arm extended and with a smile that illumined his rugged face,
giving it a charm that only those who actually saw it could
understand or appreciate, he began his speech in clear, distinct tones that carried to quite a distance. At first his
voice trembled slightly, but speedily recovered, and amid a
profound silence the audience heard the words that were
uttered by President Lincoln.

"It seemed that he had but started speaking when, with
both arms extended, as if in benediction, he finished and retired without a change in his solemn countenance. No one
realized that he had finished, evidently expecting a much
longer effort; and the awe-struck people, apparently deeply
moved, gave no sign of approval or appreciation. That was
the way it appeared to those around me and to myself.

"The profound silence which attended the speech continued; not a sound was heard for a minute or two; then

everyone began turning to his neighbors, looking into their faces, and making such comments as, 'Did he finish? Was it not a grand speech, but so short!'

"Though Everett, Seward and others on the platform shook Mr. Lincoln's hand, he quickly took his seat, evidently sorely disappointed that the people had given no sign of any kind as to the effect of the speech."

22. *Joseph L. Gilbert*

Joseph L. Gilbert, of Philadelphia, the newspaper man who reported the Gettysburg Address for the Associated Press, told the story of it at the National Shorthand Reporters' Association in August, 1917:

"On November 19, 1863, when the great President delivered his immortal address at the dedication of the National Cemetery at Gettysburg, I was present as the reporter for the Associated Press Agency. He had not been known to prepare his speeches in advance, and as he was expected to speak extempore, I was relied upon to take shorthand notes of his remarks.

"The battlefield, on that sombre autumn day, was enveloped in gloom. Nature seemed to veil her face in sorrow for the awful tragedy enacted there. The recently closed graves, the blood-drenched earth, the spectral glare of blazing bonfires recalling the army bivouacs of four months before, the over-hanging clouds in whose shadows the darkness on Cemetery Hill became absolutely funereal, the mournful sighing of the wind on a typical November day,—all these emphasized the melancholy spirit of the occasion. A profound silence reigned. The ten thousand spectators, apparently depressed by a realization of the horrors of war and the dangers that had threatened their homes, were as quiet and inanimate as statues; and, excepting a few acclamations when the President arrived, the silence remained unbroken throughout the day.

"Upon a rude platform on the crest of the hill were assembled, with President Lincoln, a host of officials, civil and military, including the Governors of the eighteen states whose citizen soldiery had taken part in the conflict on the Union side. A sea of upturned faces covered the slope in front. The ceremonies of dedication were solemn and impressive. The oration by Edward Everett gave a minute account of the three days' battle, discussed the rebellion, combated the fallacy of States Rights dogma, that the States are the principals and the National Government a mere agency, and championed the principle of Nationality. My notes give the full text of the oration, but they are too voluminous for insertion here.

"President Lincoln then came forward. I stood immediately in front of him and was impressed by his apparent excellent physical condition. His face, fringed by a newly grown beard, was more rounded and less care worn and haggard looking than formerly. He stood for a moment with hands clasped and head bowed in an attitude of mourning—a personification of the sorrow and sympathy of the nation. Adjusting his old-fashioned spectacles, a pair with arms reaching to his temples, he produced from the pocket of his Prince Albert coat several sheets of paper from which he read slowly and feelingly. His marvelous voice, careering in fullness of utterance and clearness of tone, was perfectly audible on the outskirts of the crowd. He made no gestures nor attempts at display, and none were needed. Fascinated by his intense earnestness and depth of feeling, I unconsciously stopped taking notes and looked up at him as he glanced from his manuscript with a far away look in his eyes as if appealing from the few thousands before him to the invisible audience of countless millions whom his words were to reach. No one of the many orators whom, in after years, I heard repeat the address ever made it sparkle with light and meaning as its great author did.

"When he began speaking the President had comparatively few hearers, as hundreds who had come to hear him, wearied by Everett's two-hour oration, had wandered away. But his powerful voice speedily recalled the wanderers. Spell-bound with the majestic personality of the great man of whom they had heard so much and now saw for the first time, the multitude stood mute—many with uncovered heads—listening reverently as to an inspired oracle but seemingly unconscious of the spiritual excellence and moral grandeur of the great patriot's imperishable words. It was not a demonstrative nor even an appreciative audience. Narratives of the scene have described the tumultuous outbursts of enthusiasm accompanying the President's utterances. I heard none. There were no outward manifestations of feeling. His theme did not invite holiday applause, a cemetery was not the place for it, and he did not pause to receive it.

"Lincoln wrote the address in Gettysburg at the residence of Judge Davis Wills, where he was a guest for a few hours. None of his attendants, not even his Secretary (Hay), knew of its preparation in advance of its delivery. At the Wills' mansion the President asked for the use of a private room and some writing material, remarking, 'I suppose I will be expected to make some remarks out at the Cemetery this afternoon.' His request was complied with, and in less than an hour he completed the address from rough notes made by him on the train from Washington and others he had made, several weeks earlier, when a request from the Dedication Committee 'to say a few words' was transmitted to him by Governor Curtin. The letter sheets from which he read were from Judge Wills' office. Before the dedication ceremonies closed, the President's manuscript was copied with his permission; and as the press report was made from a copy no transcript from shorthand notes was necessary."

23. *Captain Oliver Goldsmith*

In the Chicago *Journal* of November 19, 1913, just fifty years after the event, Captain Oliver Goldsmith, of the Fifth New York Regiment, which furnished the guard for the President from Baltimore to Gettysburg, said:

"Lincoln's deep, powerful voice could be heard by every one. He made few gestures. I have been asked whether there was any applause at the ceremony. There was not. It was a solemn occasion. As he resumed his seat, not a sound could be heard. It seemed as if the throng held its breath for many seconds."

24. *Honorable S. S. Warner*

I give from memory the story of the Gettysburg Address as I heard it from the Honorable S. S. Warner, at one time State Treasurer of Ohio. He said, in substance:

"My first impression as Lincoln rose was of his great stature. The next was the high pitch and thin quality of his voice as compared with the bulk of the man. But while his voice was thin and high, it carried well, and he was heard distinctly, I should think, from the very first. It took the people a moment to adjust their position, for there had been some scattering during the long oration of Mr. Everett.

"My next surprise was at his intonation. It had not occurred to me that he would speak like a Kentuckian, but he did, and his slow, careful enunciation made it the more apparent. I remember especially the long 'o' in his preposition 'to.' He said 'dedicated toe the proposition,' 'we have come toe dedicate a portion of that field.'

"My next feeling was one of complete surprise at his stopping. It seemed to me and I think to the audience generally that he had just begun. I could hardly believe my eyes when I saw him taking his seat.

"Was there applause? There may have been a little. I am not sure. I should say that he stopped before his audience was in full sympathy with him, before they had got past noticing the little oddities, and lost themselves in what he was saying. I would not say they failed to applaud because they thought poorly of what he said, but that they were just beginning to get interested, and were too surprised to applaud. If there had been much applause I am confident I should have remembered it."

25. E. W. Hart

"I was born June 2, 1849, in York County, Pennsylvania, twenty-five miles from Gettysburg. I was fourteen years and one month of age at the time of the battle. I wanted to go but had a weakness that made me deathly sick about once in six weeks. I outgrew that trouble and am now past seventy-seven. When we learned that Lincoln was to speak at Gettysburg on November 19th, father said he would go and take me. We arrived in Gettysburg early in the afternoon of the 18th. We visited the cemetery about three o'clock in the afternoon. They were burying the dead. There were drays piled high with boxes. Several pits were dug where bodies were to be buried.

"The next day I was on the ground in good time. By ten o'clock that seventeen acres had hundreds of people waiting for the parade. It was thought they would come in by the main entrance, but they came in by the west. I was standing on a pile of dirt and when he came in sight I yelled, 'There he comes.' As the crowd moved forward toward the platform, many fell into the pits. I wanted to shake his hand. When he got off his horse, I tried to get near, but two guards pushed me away. I got around in front about thirty feet from him a little to his right.

"When Everett sat down, Lincoln rose. There was applause when he rose to speak. His right hand was between me and his breast and he held his paper in his right hand. He did not read closely. Every time he raised his hand to look at his paper, I could see the sheet extending about an inch and a half above his hand and a little more below. The paper looked crumpled at the sides as if he had carried it in his pocket.

"Lincoln waited for the applause to settle before he began. Then he spoke a few sentences and again waited for the applause. This he did several times. At the close the applause was wild and frantic. A six-gun battery opened fire and they were fine for noise. The battery was a little to the left and south. I did not see a dozen soldiers except those of the battery.

"I am not in sympathy with the idea that no one knew the value of that speech. I am surprised to find people differing in a matter that is so plain to me. I may not be long here, but when I go, I shall think that I am giving the correct story of that address.

"I have made a little diagram of the platform and the place where I stood. Father worked his way around the corner of the platform and at the close climbed up. I saw him and soon was with him. We worked our way through

the crowd and shook hands with the President. Mr. Lincoln reached in front of two men to take my hand.

"I lived with my father until I was twenty-nine and then moved to Dakota and took up land. I now have been in California fifteen years. I have told this story many times, but since leaving Pennsylvania have met but one who was present at Gettysburg when Lincoln spoke. He was a soldier. We met here in California in a park. We had a very happy visit and it seemed to me very pleasant to meet someone who, like myself, heard Lincoln that day at Gettysburg."

26. Mrs. R. J. Belt

President Lincoln, who was very fond of little girls, would have been interested in knowing how one little girl remembered his address. Mrs. R. J. Belt gives this story:

"You have asked if I remember the Battle of Gettysburg. I do remember it and many things that happened during the days just before the battle. What exciting days they were! The raid into Pennsylvania caused a great stir in our little village of Wellsville, York Co., and many things were set in motion. Day and night men were passing through the village trying to find places where their horses would be safe from the terrible Rebels. The bridge at Harrisburg twenty-two miles away had been burned so they could not get their horses on the other side of the Susquehanna River. The next best thing was to hide them in the mountain about three miles north of the village. Small bands of colored people began to appear having come all the way from Hagerstown. They were panic striken and wanted to get as far away as possible from the larger towns.

"The Rebels were in Carlisle eighteen miles away, in Hanover, where Kilpatrick had a skirmish with them, and in York. Their presence in the southern part of York County was the signal for the burning of the bridge at Columbia thus cutting off another route eastward across the Susquehanna. We could see the reflection of the burning bridge and thought they were burning York.

"Of course we were much excited and expected soon to see the Rebels come through our village. Horses by this time were not seen anywhere for they were thought to be all safely hidden in the mountain.

"One morning when I was at the spring-house putting the milk away, the boy who was helping me said, 'There come the "Greybacks." ' I looked and sure enough there were four men on horseback. We locked the spring-house and hurried up to the village to tell the news.

"Our village was not on one of the main roads but between the two main roads leading from York on the south to Carlisle and Harrisburg to the north. These roads were known locally as the State Road (about one mile south of Wellsville) and the Old York Road (about two miles north). These roads in reality divide at Dover seven miles south of Wellsville and run almost parallel about two to four miles apart meeting again at Dillsburg seven miles to the north. On these two roads many detachments of the main Confederate army moved north. They seemed to be in a great hurry all day. Wherever we looked we would see them in parties of two and four combing the countryside for horses. The ones hidden in the mountain were all taken. They did not enter any houses but kept on the move. It was from them that we learned that the command of the Union army had been given to Meade, for we had had no mail for days.

"In the evening when I came up from milking, the village was deserted, not a soul was to be seen. At last an old woman came to her door and told me and the boy who was with me that everyone had gone up to the State Road to see our own army pass along. We could not miss that, and so we started for the mile walk. We found the village people, but no army. They had gone another way to Gettysburg. After staying there until twelve o'clock we all decided to go home and to bed, glad to know that the Rebels had passed and that our soldiers were after them. We did not have to wait long before we heard the cannonading of the battle for we were only twenty miles away.

"Later in the summer I was made very happy when told I could go to the dedication of the cemetery. We were fourteen miles from any railroad and I think at that time there was only one railroad into Gettysburg, a branch of the Northern Central from Hanover Junction. This route was too far around for us, so we went in a big jack-wagon with four horses driven with check lines, the same wagon that had been used all through the Lincoln campaign to carry the Wide-awakes. We called it the Great Eastern after the steamship. It held from twenty-five to thirty people and was fixed with seats running the length of the wagon. On these seats were folded our bedding for we expected to stay in Gettysburg all night. We also took provisions along. We started about half past three in the morning. It was very dark and the roads then were not as they are now and a few miles from Gettysburg as we were going through a strip of woodland we straddled a stump and broke the tongue of our wagon. We all had to get out and walk into a small town nearby where we could get it fixed. While there, team after team passed us, all going in the same direction and for the same purpose. By the time the tongue was repaired day was breaking and we were glad to be on our way. When we got to Gettys-

burg the men had to look for a place for us to stay. They
soon found a home that was glad to take us in for a consideration. There we stored our bedding and our baskets
and then we went out to go over the battle field.

"That evening some man of note made an address in a
church. I have forgotten who it was, but it really made
no impression on me for Lincoln was our idol and he was
the one we wanted to see and hear.

"The next morning there was a para . and Lincoln was
in it. I carry the memory of his bow and smile all these
years.

"In the afternoon we went to the cemetery to hear him.
I may be mistaken about the time, but I know I was in the
crowd not far from the speakers' stand. The men of our
party were seated on the edge of the stand with their feet
hanging down. When I saw the movie of Lincoln there
was no one sitting on the edge of the platform in the Gettysburg scene and it did not look right. I should have liked to
have told the producers that there should have been men
seated all around the edge of that platform.

"There I stood through that long speech of Everett's
waiting to hear Lincoln. At last Lincoln rose, there was
tremendous applause, and then he began and made such a
short speech that every one seemed to think there was some
mistake and that he was stopping before he was through.
I heard our men talking about it and they all seemed to be
disappointed. What he said was not appreciated at the
time. It was not until after it was read in the papers that
our people began to realize that a great deal had been said
in a few words.

"What followed is a blank to me. I remember nothing
of the trip home; I may have slept for I had had two very
strenuous days. The main thing to me was that I had seen
and heard Lincoln, nothing else counted.

"Of all that were in our party I, a woman of seventy-nine, am so far as I know the only one now living."

27. *Honorable Ward Hill Lamon*

Ward Hill Lamon, Lincoln's close friend, Marshal of the District of Columbia, who had charge of the special train that conveyed Lincoln to Gettysburg, and who introduced him there to the audience, told this story:

"A day or two before the dedication of the National Cemetery at Gettysburg, Mr. Lincoln told me that he would be expected to make a speech on the occasion; that he was extremely busy and had no time for preparation; that he greatly feared he would not be able to acquit himself with credit, much less to fill the measure of public expectation. From his hat—the usual receptacle for his private notes and memoranda—he drew a sheet of foolscap, one side of which was closely written with what he informed me was a memorandum of s intended address. This he read to me, first remarking t it was not at all satisfactory to him. It proved to be in stance, if not in exact words, what was afterwards prin as his famous Gettysburg speech.

"After its delivery on the day of commemoration, he expressed deep regret that he had not prepared it with greater care. He said to me on the stand, immediately after concluding the speech: 'Lamon, that speech won't *scour!* It is a flat failure, and the people are disappointed.' (The word 'scour' he often used in expressing his positive conviction that a thing lacked merit, or would not stand the test of close criticism or the wear of time.) He seemed deeply concerned about what the people might think of his address; more deeply, in fact, than I had ever seen him on any public occasion. His frank and regretful condemnation of his effort, and more especially his manner of expressing that regret, struck me as somewhat remarkable; and my own impression was deepened by the fact that the orator of the day, Mr. Everett, and Secretary Seward both coincided with Mr. Lincoln in his unfavorable view of its merits.

"The occasion was solemn, impressive, and grandly historic. The people, it is true, stood apparently spell-bound; and the vast throng was hushed and awed into profound silence while Mr. Lincoln delivered his brief speech. But it seemed to him that this silence and attention to his words arose more from the solemnity of the ceremonies and the awful scenes which gave rise to them, than from anything he had said. He believed that the speech was a failure. He thought so at the time, and he never referred to it afterwards, in conversation with me, without some expression of unqualified regret that he had not made the speech better in every way.

"On the platform from which Mr. Lincoln delivered his address, and only a moment after it was concluded, Mr. Seward turned to Mr. Everett and asked him what he thought of the President's speech. Mr. Everett replied, 'It is not what I expected from him. I am disappointed.' Then in his turn Mr. Everett asked, 'What do you think of it, Mr. Seward?' The response was, 'He has made a failure, and I am sorry for it. His speech was not equal to him.' Mr. Seward then turned to me and asked, 'Mr. Marshal, what do you think of it?' I answered, 'I am sorry to say that it does not impress me as one of his great speeches.'

"In the face of these facts it has been repeatedly published that this speech was received by the audience with loud demonstrations of approval; that 'amid the tears, sobs, and cheers it produced in the excited throng, the orator of the day, Mr. Everett, turned to Mr. Lincoln grasped his hand and exclaimed, "I congratulate you on your success!" adding in a transport of heated enthusiasm, "Ah, Mr. President, how gladly would I give my hundred pages to be the author of your twenty lines!"' Nothing of the kind occurred. It is a slander on Mr. Everett, an injustice to Mr. Lincoln, and a falsification of history. Mr. Everett could not have used the words attributed to him, in the face of his own condemnation of the speech uttered a moment before, without subjecting himself to the charge of being a toady and a hypocrite; and he was neither the one nor the other.

"As a matter of fact, the silence during the delivery of the speech, and the lack of hearty demonstrations of approval immediately afterward, were taken by Mr. Lincoln as certain proof that it was not well received. In that opinion we all shared. If any person then present saw, or thought he saw, the marvelous beauties of that wonderful speech, as intelligent men in all lands now see and acknowledge them, his super-abundant caution closed his lips and stayed his pen. Mr. Lincoln said to me after our return to Washington, 'I tell you, Hill, that speech fell on the audience like a wet blanket. I am distressed about it. I ought to have prepared it with more care.' Such continued to be his opinion of that most wonderful of all his platform addresses up to the time of his death.

"I state it as a fact, and without fear of contradiction, that this famous Gettysburg speech was not regarded by the audience to whom it was addressed, or by the press and the people of the United States, as a production of extraordinary merit, nor was it commented on as such until after the death of its author. Those who look thoughtfully into the history of the matter must own that Mr. Lincoln was, on that occasion, 'wiser than he knew.' He was wiser than his audience, wiser than the great scholars and orators who were associated with him in the events of that solemn day. He had unconsciously risen to a height above the level of even the 'cultured thought' of that period."

28. Colonel Clark E. Carr

Colonel Clark E. Carr, who represented Illinois on the Gettysburg Cemetery Commission, and who sat near to Mr. Lincoln as he delivered his address, thus related the story of the occasion, including that of the invitation sent to the President and the effect of the address as Colonel Carr heard it:

"When the President thus appeared it was the first opportunity the people really had to see him. There was the usual craning of necks, the usual exclamations of 'Down in front!' the usual crowding to get places to see, and much confusion. He waited patiently for the audience to become quiet, and there was absolute silence while he spoke. He began in those high, clarion tones, which the people of Illinois had so often heard, to which he held to the close. His was a voice that, when he made an effort, could reach a great multitude, and he always tried to make every one hear. He held in his left hand two or three pages of manuscript, toward which he glanced but once. He spoke with deliberation, but can not have continued more than three or four, some said two, minutes.

"A moment's reflection will convince any one that before the great multitude of people, nearly all of whom were standing, could have prepared themselves to listen intelligently—before they had, I may say, become poised, before their thoughts had become sufficiently centered upon the speaker to take up his line of thought and follow him, he had finished and returned to his seat.

"So short a time was Mr. Lincoln before them that the people could scarcely believe their eyes when he disappeared from their view. They were almost dazed. They could not possibly, in so short a time, mentally grasp the ideas that were conveyed, nor even their substance. Time and again expressions of disappointment were made to me. Many persons said to me that they would have supposed that on such a great occasion the President would have made a speech. Every one thought, as expressed by Mr. Wills four days later (to which reference has been made), that instead of Mr. Lincoln's delivering an address, he only made a very few 'dedicatory remarks.'

"We on the platform heard every word. And what did we hear? A dozen commonplace sentences, scarcely one of which contained anything new, anything that when stated was not self-evident.

"I am aware, because I noted it at the time, that in the Associated Press report, which appeared in the morning papers, there were the punctuations of 'Applause' and 'long continued applause,' according to the invariable custom of those times. Except as he concluded, I did not observe it, and at the close the applause was not especially marked. The occasion was too solemn for any kind of boisterous demonstration."

29. John G. Nicolay

After Nicolay and Hay had published their *Abraham Lincoln: A History*, Mr. Nicolay prepared for the *Century Magazine* an account of the actual writing of the manuscript of the Gettysburg Address which Lincoln held in his hand when he delivered it. John Hay had no part, apparently, in the work of preparation, but Nicolay was present, and his story, considerably abbreviated, is convincing:

"It was after the breakfast hour on the morning of the 19th that the writer, Mr. Lincoln's private secretary, went to the upper room in the house of Mr. Wills which Mr. Lincoln occupied, to report for duty, and remained with the President while he finished writing the Gettysburg address, during the short leisure he could utilize for this purpose before being called to take his place in the procession, which was announced on the program to move promptly at ten o'clock.

"There is neither record, evidence, nor well-founded tradition that Mr. Lincoln did any writing, or made any notes, on the journey between Washington and Gettysburg. The train consisted of four passenger-coaches, and either composition or writing would have been extremely troublesome amid all the movement, the noise, the conversation, the greetings, and the questionings which ordinary courtesy required him to undergo in these surroundings; but still worse would have been the rockings and joltings of the train, rendering writing virtually impossible. Mr. Lincoln carried in his pocket the autograph manuscript of so much of his address as he had written at Washington the day before. Precisely what that was the reader can now see by turning to the facsimile reproduction of the original draft, which is for the first time printed and made public in this article. It fills one page of the letter-paper at that time habitually used in the Executive Mansion, containing the plainly printed blank heading; both paper and print giving convincing testimony to the simple and economical business methods then prevailing in the White House.

"This portion of the manuscript begins with the line 'Four score and seven years ago,' and ends 'It is rather for us the living,' etc. The whole of this first page—nineteen lines—is written in ink in the President's strong clear hand, without blot or erasure; and the last line is in the following form: 'It is rather for us the living to stand here,' the last three words being, like the rest, in ink. From the fact that this sentence is incomplete, we may infer that at the time of writing it in Washington the remainder of the sentence was also written in ink on another piece of paper.

But when, at Gettysburg on the morning of the ceremonies, Mr. Lincoln finished his manuscript, he used a lead pencil, with which he crossed out the last three words of the first page, and wrote above them in pencil 'we here be dedica,' at which point he took up a new half sheet of paper—not white letter-paper as before, but a bluish-gray foolscap of large size with wide lines, habitually used by him for long or formal documents, and on this he wrote, all in pencil, the remainder of the word, and of the first draft of the address, comprising a total of nine lines and a half.

"The time occupied in this final writing was probably about an hour, for it is not likely that he left the breakfast table before nine o'clock, and the formation of the procession began at ten. The grand marshal of the day had made preparations for an imposing procession, and to this end, instead of carriages ordinarily used on such occasions, had arranged that the President and other dignitaries should ride to the grounds on horseback. We learn from the newspaper reports that at about ten o'clock the President issued from Mr. Wills's house attired in black, with white gauntlets upon his hands; that as soon as he had mounted he was besieged by a crowd eager to shake hands with him, and that the marshals had some difficulty in inducing the people to desist and allow him to sit in peace upon his horse. Secretaries Seward, Blair, and Usher also mounted horses, as did others of the official retinue. There were the usual delays incident to such occasions, rather aggravated in this instance by the fact that intense curiosity to see the battle-field had already drawn thither the larger part of the great crowd in the village without waiting to join the procession; so that for want of numbers the pageant did not make the imposing display which had been anticipated.

"The procession, however, finally moved, and at about eleven o'clock the Presidential party reached the platform.

Mr. Everett, the orator of the day, arrived fully half an hour later, and there was still further waiting before the military bodies and civic spectators could be properly ranged and stationed. It was therefore fully noon before Mr. Everett began his address, after which, for two hours, he held the assembled multitude in rapt attention with his eloquent description and argument, his polished diction, his carefully studied and practised delivery.

"When he had concluded, and the band had performed the usual musical interlude, President Lincoln rose to fill the part assigned him in the program. It was entirely natural for every one to expect that this would consist of a few perfunctory words, the mere formality of official dedication. There is every probability that the assemblage regarded Mr. Everett as the mouthpiece, the organ of expression of the thought and feeling of the hour, and took it for granted that Mr. Lincoln was there as a mere official figure-head, the culminating decoration, so to speak, of the elaborately planned pageant of the day. They were therefore totally unprepared for what they heard, and could not immediately realize that *his* words, and not those of the carefully selected orator, were to carry the concentrated thought of the occasion like a trumpet-peal to farthest posterity.

"The newspaper records indicate that when Mr. Lincoln began to speak, he held in his hand the manuscript first draft of his address which he had finished only a short time before. But it is the distinct recollection of the writer, who sat within a few feet of him, that he did not read from the written pages, though that impression was naturally left upon many of his auditors. That it was not a mere mechanical reading is, however, more definitely confirmed by the circumstance that Mr. Lincoln did not deliver the address in the exact form in which his first draft is written. It was taken down in shorthand by the reporter for the

'Associated Press,' telegraphed to the principal cities, and printed on the following morning in the leading newspapers.

"It would also appear that a few, but only a very few, independent shorthand reports or abstracts were made by other correspondents.

"In addition to that from Mr. Wills, other requests soon came to him for autograph copies. The number he made, and for what friends, cannot now be confidently stated, though it was probably half a dozen or more, all written by him with painstaking care to correspond word for word with his revision. If in any respect they differed from each other, it was due to accident, and against his intention. At this period of the war unusual efforts were being made to collect funds for the use of the Sanitary Commission in sending supplies and relief in various forms to sick and wounded soldiers in army hospitals and camps in the South. During that autumn the President had given the original manuscript of his final Emancipation Proclamation to a fair held at Chicago for this object, at the close of which the manuscript was sold at auction for the handsome sum of three thousand dollars. The managers of other fairs naturally wished to take similar advantage of his personal popularity. Thus Mr. Everett wrote him under date of January 30, 1864:

" 'I shall have the honor of forwarding to you by express, to-day or on Monday next, a copy of the authorized edition, my Gettysburg address and of the remarks made by yourself, and the other matters connected with the ceremonial of the dedication of the Cemetery. It appeared, owing to unavoidable delays, only yesterday.

" 'I have promised to give the manuscript of my address to Mrs. Governor Fish of New York, who is at the head of the Ladies' Committee of the Metropolitan fair. It would add very greatly to its value if I could bind up with it the manuscript of your dedicatory remarks, if you happen to have preserved it.

" 'I would further venture to request, that you would allow me also to bind up in the volume the very obliging letter of the 20th November, 1863, which you did me the favor to write me. I shall part with it with much reluctance, and I shrink a little from the apparent indelicacy of giving some publicity to a letter highly complimentary to myself. But as its insertion would greatly enhance the value of the volume when sold at the fair, I shall, if I have your kind permission, waive all other considerations.'

"To this request Mr. Lincoln replied under date of February 4:

" 'Yours of January 30th was received four days ago; and since then the address mentioned has arrived. Thank you for it. I send herewith the manuscript of my remarks at Gettysburg, which, with my note to you of November 20th, you are at liberty to use for the benefit of our soldiers, as you have requested.'

"Baltimore also was being stirred by the same spirit of national patriotism, and a novel attraction was planned in aid of its Soldiers' and Sailors' Fair, the opening day of which was fixed for April 18, 1864. On the 5th of February a committee consisting of the Honorable John P. Kennedy, author of 'Swallow Barn' and other novels, and Colonel Alexander Bliss, then serving on the military staff of General Schenck commanding at Baltimore, sent a circular to prominent American authors, soliciting from each a page or two of autograph manuscript to be published in facsimile in a small quarto volume and to be sold for the benefit of the fair. Some time in the month of February George Bancroft, the historian, who was in Washington, made verbal application to the President, on their behalf, for an autograph copy of his Gettysburg address, to be included in the volume. Mr. Lincoln wrote and sent them a copy; and when it was discovered that it was written on both sides of a letter sheet, and on that account was not available to be used in the process of lithographing, he made them a second copy, written only on one side of the letter pages. This was sent to the committee on March 11, 1864, and Mr. Bancroft was permitted to keep the first; which appears recently to have passed, with other papers of the great historian, into the possession of the Lenox Library. The Baltimore committee had the other duly lithographed and printed in their volume, and it was sold at the fair. The first facsimile in the book of two hundred pages is that of the 'Star-Spangled Banner,' the second, Abraham Lincoln's Gettysburg address, and the last, 'Home, Sweet Home'; while between them are autograph specimen-pages from the writings of nearly a hundred American authors. It is this Baltimore facsimile which by frequent photographs, and therefore exact reproduction, has properly become the standard text, and size. The originals of the whole collection are still in the possession of Colonel Alexander Bliss, of Washington, D. C., who, as one of the committee, conducted the correspondence in gathering it.

"Having made a comparison of the President's original draft with the Associated Press report printed in the newspapers, it will now be interesting to compare the Associated Press report with the final revision. A careful examination shows that there were in all thirteen changes; that seven of these are a mere return to, or restoration of, words in the

first draft, correcting the errors which evidently occurred
in the transmission by telegraph and the newspaper type-
setting, namely: 'are met' changed back to 'have come';
'the' changed back to 'a'; 'of' changed back to 'for'; 'power'
changed back to 'poor power'; 'the' changed back to 'these';
'governments' changed back to 'government'; 'and' omitted
from the last sentence, as at first.

"The other six changes are the President's own deliberate revision, namely: 'upon' changed to 'on'; 'it'
changed to 'that field'; 'they have' changed to 'they who
fought here have'; 'carried on' changed to 'advanced';
'they here gàve' changed to 'they gave'; and the phrase
'shall under God' transposed to read 'under God shall.'

"By this comparative analysis we have clearly before
us in every detail the whole process of growth and perfection which the Gettysburg address underwent from the
original draft to the final artistic form in which, after
mature reflection, he desired it should stand. That this
amplifying process was important and valuable in a literary
point of view is evident. But if we count the changes, five
in number, between the original draft and the spoken address, and six more between the spoken address and the
final revision, and then study the nature and quality of the
changes, we see that in the elements of brevity and force
of statement, philosophic breadth of thought, and terse,
vigorous expression—in short, in everything except mere
rhetorical finish, the first draft is as complete and worthy of
admiration as the final revision."

CHAPTER XXII

The Oration of Honorable Edward Everett

THIS oration is printed from the manuscript as revised by Doctor Everett after the delivery of the address, and as printed in the Official Report of the Cemetery Commission in 1864. It contains the best contemporary account of the battle, based on special descriptions prepared for him by General Meade and other participants, and revised after Everett's own three days' study of the field. It will be noted that Everett, in common with writers so near the event, had not as yet conceived of the three days' struggle as constituting a single battle; he spoke of "the battles of Gettysburg."

"Standing beneath this serene sky, overlooking these broad fields now reposing from the labors of the waning year, the mighty Alleghenies dimly towering before us, the graves of our brethren beneath our feet, it is with hesitation that I raise my poor voice to break the eloquent silence of God and Nature. But the duty to which you have called me must be performed;—grant me, I pray you, your indulgence and your sympathy.

"It was appointed by law in Athens, that the obsequies of the citizens who fell in battle should be performed at the public expense, and in the most honorable manner. Their bones were carefully gathered up from the funeral pyre, where their bodies were consumed, and brought home to the city. There, for three days before the interment, they lay in state, beneath tents of honor, to receive the votive offerings of friends and relatives,—flowers, weapons, precious ornaments, painted vases, (wonders of art, which after two thousand years adorn the museums of modern Europe,)—the last tributes of surviving affection. Ten coffins of funeral cypress received the honorable deposit, one for each of the tribes of the city, and an eleventh in memory of the unrecognized, but not therefore unhonored, dead, and of those whose remains could not be recovered. On the fourth day the mournful procession was formed; mothers, wives, sisters, daughters led the way, and to them it was permitted by the simplicity of ancient manners to utter aloud their lamentations for the beloved and the lost; the male relatives and friends of the deceased followed; citizens and strangers closed the train. Thus marshalled, they moved to the place of interment in that famous Cera-micus, the most beautiful suburb of Athens, which had been adorned by Cimon, the son of Miltiades, with walks and fountains and columns,—whose groves were filled with altars, shrines, and temples,—whose gardens were kept forever green by the streams from the neighboring hills, and shaded with the trees sacred to Minerva and coeval with the foundation of the city,—whose circuit enclosed

" 'the olive Grove of Academe,
Plato's retirement, where the Attic bird
Trilled his thick-warbled note the summer long,'—

whose pathways gleamed with the monuments of the illustrious dead, the work of the most consummate masters that ever gave life to marble. There, beneath the over-arching plane-trees, upon a lofty stage erected for the pur-pose, it was ordained that a funeral oration should be pronounced by some citizen of Athens, in the presence of the assembled multitude.

"Such were the tokens of respect required to be paid at Athens to the memory of those who had fallen in the cause of their country. For those alone who fell at Marathon a special honor was reserved. As the battle fought upon that immortal field was distinguished from all others in Grecian history for its influence over the fortunes of Hellas,—as it depended upon the event of that day whether Greece should live, a glory and a light to all coming time, or should expire, like the meteor of a moment; so the honors awarded to its martyr-heroes were such as were bestowed by Athens on no other occasion. They alone of all her sons were entombed upon the spot which they had forever rendered famous. Their names were inscribed upon ten pillars, erected upon the monumental tumulus which covered their ashes, (where after six hundred years, they were read by the traveler Pausanias,) and although the columns, beneath the hand of time and barbaric violence, have long since disappeared, the venerable mound still marks the spot where they fought and fell,—

" 'That battle-field where Persia's victim horde
First bowed beneath the brunt of Hellas' sword.'

"And shall I, fellow citizens, who, after an interval of twenty-three centuries, a youthful prilgrim from the world unknown to ancient Greece, have wandered over that illustrious plain, ready to put off the shoes from off my feet, as one that stands on holy ground,—who have gazed with respectful emotion on the mound which still protects the dust of those who rolled back the tide of Persian invasion, and rescued the land of popular liberty, of letters, and of arts, from the ruthless foe,—stand unmoved over the graves of our dear brethren, who so lately, on three of those all-important days which decide a nation's history,— days on whose issue it depended whether this august republican Union, founded by some of the wisest statesmen that ever lived, cemented with the blood of some of the purest patriots that ever died, should perish or endure,— rolled back the tide of an invasion, not less unprovoked, not less ruthless, than that which came to plant the dark banner of Asiatic despotism and slavery on the free soil of Greece? Heaven forbid! And could I prove so insensible to every prompting of patriotic duty and affection, not only would you, fellow citizens, gathered many of you from distant States, who have come to take part in these pious offices of gratitude—you, respected fathers, brethren, matrons, sisters, who surround me—cry out for shame, but the forms of brave and patriotic men who fill these honored graves would heave with indignation beneath the sod.

"We have assembled, friends, fellow citizens, at the invitation of the Executive of the great central State of Pennsylvania, seconded by the Governors of seventeen other loyal States of the Union, to pay the last tribute of respect to the brave men, who, in the hard fought battles of the first, second and third days of July last, laid down their lives for the country on these hill sides and the plains before us, and whose remains have been gathered into the Cemetery which we consecrate this day. As my eye ranges over the fields whose sods were so lately moistened by the blood of gallant and loyal men, I feel, as never before, how truly it was said of old, that it is sweet and becoming to die for one's country. I feel as never before, how justly, from the dawn of history to the present time, men have paid the homage of their gratitude and admiration to the memory of those who nobly sacrificed their lives, that their fellow men may live in safety and in honor. And if this tribute were ever due, when, to whom, could it be more justly paid than to those whose last resting place we this day commend to the blessing of Heaven and of men?

"For consider, my friends, what would have been the consequences to the country, to yourselves, and to all you hold dear, if those who sleep beneath our feet, and their gallant comrades who survive to serve their country on other fields of danger, had failed in their duty on those memorable days. Consider what, at this moment, would be the condition of the United States, if that noble army of the Potomac, instead of gallantly and for the second time beating back the tide of invasion from Maryland and Pennsylvania, had been itself driven from these well contested heights, thrown back in confusion on Baltimore, or trampled down, discomfited, scattered to the four winds. What, in that sad event, would not have been the fate of the Monumental city, of Harrisburg, of Philadelphia, of Washington, the capital of the Union, each and every one of which would have lain at the mercy of the enemy, accordingly as it might have pleased him, spurred by passion, flushed with victory, and confident of continued success, to direct his course?

"For this we must bear in mind, it is one of the great lessons of the war, indeed of every war, that it is impossible for a people without military organization, inhabiting the cities, towns, and villages of an open country, including, of course, the natural proportion of non-combatants of either sex, and of every age, to withstand the inroad of a veteran army. What defence can be made by the inhabitants of villages mostly built of wood, of cities unprotected by walls, nay, by a population of men, however high-toned and resolute, whose aged parents demand their care, whose wives and children are clustering about them, against the charge of the war-horse whose neck is clothed with thunder—against flying artillery and batteries of rifled cannon planted on every commanding eminence—against the onset of trained veterans led by skilful chiefs? No, my friends, army must be met by army, battery by battery, squadron by squadron; and the shock of organized thousands must be encountered by the firm breasts and valiant arms of other thousands, as well organized and as skilfully led. It is no reproach, therefore, to the unarmed population of the country to say, that we owe it to the brave men who sleep in their beds of honor before us, and to their gallant surviving associates, not merely that your fertile fields, my friends of Pennsylvania and Maryland, were redeemed from the presence of the invader, but that your capitals were not given up to threatened plunder, perhaps laid in ashes, Washington seized by the enemy, and a blow struck at the heart of the nation.

"Who that hears me has forgotten the thrill of joy that ran through the country on the 4th of July—auspicious day for the glorious tidings, and rendered still more so by the simultaneous fall of Vicksburg—when the telegraph flashed through the land the assurance from the President of the United States that the army of the Potomac, under General Meade, had again smitten the invader? Sure I am, that, with the ascriptions of praise that rose to Heaven from twenty millions of freemen, with the acknowledgments that breathed from patriotic lips throughout the length and breadth of America, to the surviving officers and men who had rendered the country this inestimable service, there beat in every loyal bosom a throb of tender and sorrowful gratitude to the martyrs who had fallen on the sternly contested field. Let a nation's fervent thanks make some amends for the toils and sufferings of those who survive. Would that the heartfelt tribute could penetrate these honored graves!

"In order that we may comprehend, to their full extent, our obligations to the martyrs and surviving heroes of the army of the Potomac, let us contemplate for a few moments the train of events, which culminated in the battles of the first days of July. Of this stupendous rebellion, planned, as its originators boast, more than thirty years ago, matured and prepared for during an entire generation, finally commenced because, for the first time since the adoption of the Constitution, an election of President had been effected without the votes of the South, (which retained, however, the control of the two other branches of the government,) the occupation of the national capital, with the seizure of the public archives and of the treaties with foreign powers, was an essential feature. This was, in substance, within my personal knowledge, admitted, in the winter of 1860-61, by one of the most influential leaders of the rebellion; and it was fondly thought that this object could be effected by a bold and sudden movement on the 4th of March, 1861. There is abundant proof, also, that a darker project was contemplated, if not by the responsible chiefs of the rebellion, yet by nameless ruffians, willing to play a subsidiary and murderous part in the treasonable drama. It was accordingly maintained by the Rebel emissaries in England, in the circles to which they found access, that the new American Minister ought not, when he arrived, to be received as the envoy of the United States, inasmuch as before that time Washington would be captured, and the capital of the nation and the archives and muniments of the government would be in the possession of the Confederates. In full accordance also with this threat, it was declared, by the Rebel Secretary of War, at Montgomery, in the presence of his Chief and of his colleagues, and of five thousand hearers, while the tidings of the assault on Sumter were traveling over the wires on that fatal 12th of April, 1861, that before the end of May 'the flag which then flaunted the breeze,' as he expressed it, 'would float over the dome of the Capitol at Washington.'

"At the time this threat was made, the rebellion was confined to the cotton-growing States, and it was well understood by them, that the only hope of drawing any of the other slaveholding States into the conspiracy, was in bringing about a conflict of arms, and 'firing the heart of the South' by the effusion of blood. This was declared by the Charleston press, to be the object for which Sumter was to be assaulted; and the emissaries sent from Richmond, to urge on the unhallowed work, gave the promise, that, with the first drop of blood that should be shed, Virginia would place herself by the side of South Carolina.

"In pursuance of this original plan of the leaders of the rebellion, the capture of Washington has been continually had in view, not merely for the sake of its public buildings, as the capital of the Confederacy, but as the necessary preliminary to the absorption of the border States, and for the moral effect in the eyes of Europe of possessing the metropolis of the Union.

"I allude to these facts, not perhaps enough borne in mind, as a sufficient refutation of the pretence, on the part of the Rebels, that the war is one of self-defence, waged for the right of self-government. It is in reality, a war originally levied by ambitious men in the cotton-growing States, for the purpose of drawing the slaveholding border States into the vortex of the conspiracy, first by sympathy— which, in the case of South-Eastern Virginia, North Carolina, part of Tennessee and Arkansas, succeeded—and then by force and for the purpose of subjugating Maryland, Western Virginia, Kentucky, Eastern Tennessee and Missouri; and it is a most extraordinary fact, considering the clamors of the Rebel chiefs on the subject of invasion, that not a soldier of the United States has entered the States last named, except to defend their Union-loving inhabitants from the armies and guerillas of the Rebels.

"In conformity with these designs on the city of Washington, and notwithstanding the disastrous results of the invasion of 1862, it was determined by the Rebel Government last summer to resume the offensive in that direction. Unable to force the passage of the Rappahannock, where General Hooker, notwithstanding the reverse at Chancellorsville, in May, was strongly posted, the Confederate general resorted to strategy. He had two objects in view. The first was by a rapid movement northward, and by manœuvering with a portion of his army on the east side of the Blue Ridge, to tempt Hooker from his base of operations, thus leading him to uncover the approaches to Washington, to throw it open to a raid by Stuart's cavalry, and to enable Lee himself to cross the Potomac in the neighborhood of Poolesville and thus fall upon the capital. This plan of operations was wholly frustrated. The design of the Rebel general was promptly discovered by General Hooker, and, moving with great rapidity from Fredericksburg, he preserved unbroken the inner line, and stationed the various corps of his army at all the points protecting the approach to Washington, from Centreville up to Leesburg. From this vantage-ground the Rebel general in vain attempted to draw him. In the mean time, by the vigorous operations of Pleasanton's cavalry, the cavalry of Stuart, though greatly superior in numbers, was so crippled as to be disabled from performing the part assigned it in the campaign. In this manner, General Lee's first object, namely, the defeat of Hooker's army on the south of the Potomac and a direct march on Washington, was baffled.

"The second part of the Confederate plan, which is supposed to have been undertaken in opposition to the views of General Lee, was to turn the demonstration northward into a real invasion of Maryland and Pennsylvania, in the hope, that, in this way, General Hooker would

be drawn to a distance from the capital, and that some
opportunity would occur of taking him at disadvantage,
and, after defeating his army, of making a descent upon
Baltimore and Washington. This part of General Lee's
plan, which was substantially the repetition of that of 1862,
was not less signally defeated, with what honor to the arms
of the Union the heights on which we are this day assembled will forever attest.

"Much time had been uselessly consumed by the Rebel
general in his unavailing attempts to out-manœuvre General Hooker. Although General Lee broke up from
Fredericksburg on the 3d of June, it was not till the 24th
that the main body of his army entered Maryland. Instead
of crossing the Potomac, as he had intended, east of the
Blue Ridge, he was compelled to do it at Shepherdstown
and Williamsport, thus materially deranging his entire plan
of campaign north of the river. Stuart, who had been sent
with his cavalry to the east of the Blue Ridge, to guard the
passes of the mountains, to mask the movements of Lee,
and to harass the Union general in crossing the river, having been severely handled by Pleasanton at Beverly Ford,
Aldie, and Upperville, instead of being able to retard General Hooker's advance, was driven himself away from his
connection with the army of Lee, and cut off for a fortnight
from all communication with it—a circumstance to which
General Lee, in his report, alludes more than once, with
evident displeasure. Let us now rapidly glance at the
incidents of the eventful campaign.

"A detachment from Ewell's corps, under Jenkins, had
penetrated, on the 15th of June, as far as Chambersburg.
This movement was intended at first merely as a demonstration, and as a marauding expedition for supplies. It had,
however, the salutary effect of alarming the country; and
vigorous preparations were made, not only by the General

Government, but here in Pennsylvania and in the sister States, to repel the inroad.   After two days passed at Chambersburg, Jenkins, anxious for his communications with Ewell, fell back with his plunder to Hagerstown. Here he remained for several days, and then having swept the recesses of the Cumberland valley, came down upon the eastern flank of the South mountain, and pushed his marauding parties as far as Waynesboro.   On the 22nd, the remainder of Ewell's corps crossed the river and moved up the valley.   They were followed on the 24th by Long-street and Hill, who crossed at Williamsport and Sheperds-town, and pushing up the valley, encamped at Chambersburg on the 27th.   In this way the whole rebel army, estimated at 90,000 infantry, upwards of 10,000 cavalry, and 4,000 or 5,000 artillery, making a total of 105,000 of all arms, was concentrated in Pennsylvania.

"Up to this time no report of Hooker's movements had been received by General Lee, who, having been deprived of his cavalry, had no means of obtaining information. Rightly judging, however, that no time would be lost by the Union army in the pursuit, in order to detain it on the eastern side of the mountains in Maryland and Pennsyl-vania, and thus preserve his communications by the way of Williamsport, he had, before his own arrival at Chambers-burg, directed Ewell to send detachments from his corps to Carlisle and York.   The latter detachment, under Early, passed through this place on the 26th of June.   You need not, fellow citizens of Gettysburg, that I should recall to you those moments of alarm and distress, precursors as they were of the more trying scenes which were so soon to follow.

"As soon as Gen. Hooker perceived that the advance of the Confederates into the Cumberland valley was not a mere feint to draw him away from Washington, he moved

rapidly in pursuit.   Attempts, as we have seen, were made
to harass and retard his passage across the Potomac. These
attempts were not only altogether unsuccessful, but were so
unskilfully made as to place the entire Federal army between the cavalry of Stuart and the army of Lee.   While
the latter was massed in the Cumberland valley, Stuart was
east of the mountains, with Hooker's army between, and
Gregg's cavalry in close pursuit.   Stuart was accordingly
compelled to force a march northward, which was destitute
of strategical character, and which deprived his chief of
all means of obtaining intelligence.

"Not a moment had been lost by General Hooker in the
pursuit of Lee.   The day after the Rebel army entered
Maryland, the Union army crossed the Potomac at
Edward's Ferry, and by the 28th of June lay between Harper's Ferry and Frederick.   The force of the enemy on that
day was partly at Chambersburg, and partly moving on the
Cashtown road in the direction of Gettysburg, while the detachments from Ewell's corps, of which mention has been
made, had reached the Susquehanna opposite Harrisburg
and Columbia.   That a great battle must soon be fought,
no one could doubt; but in the apparent and perhaps real
absence of plan on the part of Lee, it was impossible to
foretell the precise scene of the encounter.   Wherever
fought, consequences the most momentous hung upon the
result.

"In this critical and anxious state of affairs, General
Hooker was relieved, and General Meade was summoned
to the chief command of the army.   It appears to my un-
military judgment to reflect the highest credit upon him,
upon his predecessor, and upon the corps commanders of
the army of the Potomac, that a change could take place
in the chief command of so large a force on the eve of a
general battle—the various corps necessarily moving on

lines somewhat divergent, and all in ignorance of the enemy's intended point of concentration—and that not an hour's hesitation should ensue in the advance of any portion of the entire army.

"Having assumed the chief command on the 28th, General Meade directed his left wing, under Reynolds, upon Emmitsburg, and his right upon New Windsor, leaving General French with 11,000 men to protect the Baltimore and Ohio railroad, and convoy the public property from Harper's Ferry to Washington. Buford's cavalry was then at this place, and Kilpatrick's at Hanover, where he encountered and defeated the rear of Stuart's cavalry, who was roving the country in search of the main army of Lee. On the Rebel side, Hill had reached Fayetteville on the Cashtown road on the 28th, and was followed on the same road by Longstreet on the 29th. The eastern side of the mountain, as seen from Gettysburg, was lighted up at night by the camp-fires of the enemy's advance, and the country swarmed with his foraging parties. It was now too evident to be questioned, that the thunder-cloud, so long gathering blackness, would soon burst on some part of the devoted vicinity of Gettysburg.

"The 30th of June was a day of important preparation. At half-past eleven o'clock in the morning, General Buford passed through Gettysburg, upon a reconnoissance in force, with his cavalry, upon the Chambersburg road. The information obtained by him was immediately communicated to General Reynolds, who was, in consequence, directed to occupy Gettysburg. That gallant officer accordingly, with the First Corps, marched from Emmitsburg to within six or seven miles of this place, and encamped on the right bank of Marsh's creek. Our right wing, meantime, was moved to Manchester. On the same day the corps of Hill and Longstreet were pushed still further forward on the

Chambersburg road, and distributed in the vicinity of Marsh's creek, while a reconnoissance was made by the Confederate General Pettigrew up to a very short distance from this place.—Thus at nightfall, on the 30th of June, the greater part of the Rebel force was concentrated in the immediate vicinity of two corps of the Union army, the former refreshed by two days passed in comparative repose and deliberate preparation for the encounter, the latter separated by a march of one or two days from their supporting corps, and doubtful at what precise point they were to expect an attack.

"And now the momentous day, a day to be forever remembered in the annals of the country, arrived. Early in the morning, on the 1st of July, the conflict began. I need not say that it would be impossible for me to comprise, within the limits of the hour, such a narrative as would do anything like full justice to the all-important events of these three great days, or to the merit of the brave officers and men, of every rank, of every arm of the service, and of every loyal State, who bore their part in the tremendous struggle—alike those who nobly sacrificed their lives for their country, and those who survive, many of them scarred with honorable wounds, the objects of our admiration and gratitude. The astonishingly minute, accurate, and graphic accounts contained in the journals of the day, prepared from personal observation by reporters who witnessed the scenes, and often shared the perils which they describe, and the highly valuable "notes" of Professor Jacobs, of the University in this place, to which I am greatly indebted, will abundantly supply the deficiency of my necessarily too condensed statement.*

---

*"Besides the sources of information mentioned in the text, I have been kindly favored with a memorandum of the operations of the three days, drawn up for me by direction of Major General Meade, (anticipating the promulgation of his official report,) by one of his aids, Colonel Theodore

"General Reynolds, on arriving at Gettysburg, in the morning of the 1st, found Buford with his cavalry warmly engaged with the enemy, whom he held most gallantly in check. Hastening himself to the front, General Reynolds directed his men to be moved over the fields from the Emmitsburg road, in front of M'Millan's and Dr. Schmucker's, under cover of the Seminary Ridge. Without a moment's hesitation, he attacked the enemy, at the same time sending orders to the Eleventh Corps (General Howard's) to advance as promptly as possible. General Reynolds immediately found himself engaged with a force

---

Lyman, from whom, also, I have received other important communications relative to the campaign. I have received very valuable documents relative to the battle from Major General Halleck, Commander-in-Chief of the army, and have been much assisted in drawing up the sketch of the campaign, by the detailed reports, kindly transmitted to me in manuscript from the Adjutant General's office, of the movements of every corps of the army, for each day, after the breaking up from Fredericksburg commenced. I have derived much assistance from Colonel John B. Bachelder's oral explanations of his beautiful and minute drawing (about to be engraved) of the field of the three days' struggle. With the information derived from these sources, I have compared the statements in General Lee's official report of the campaign, dated 31st July, 1863, a well-written article, purporting to be an account of the three days' battle, in the *Richmond Enquirer* of the 22d of July, and the article on "The Battle of Gettysburg and the Campaign of Pennsylvania," by an officer, apparently a colonel in the British army, in *Blackwood's Magazine* for September. The value of the information contained in this last essay may be seen by comparing the remark under date 27th June, that 'private property is to be rigidly protected,' with the statement in the next sentence but one, that 'all the cattle and farm horses having been seized by Ewell, farm labor had come to a complete stand still.' He, also, under date of 4th July, speaks of Lee's retreat being encumbered by 'Ewell's *immense train of plunder.*' This writer informs us, that, on the evening of the 4th of July, he heard 'reports coming in from the different *Generals,* that the enemy [Meade's army] was *retiring,* and had been doing so all day long.' At a consultation at head-quarters on the 6th, between Generals Lee, Longstreet, Hill, and Wilcox, this writer was told by some one, whose name he prudently leaves in blank, that the army had no intention, at present, of retreating for good, and that some of the enemy's dispatches had been intercepted, in which the following words occur: 'The noble, but unfortunate army of the Potomac has again been obliged to retreat before superior numbers!' He does not appear to be aware, that in recording these wretched expedients, resorted to in order to keep up the spirits of Lee's army, he furnishes the most complete refutation of his own account of its good condition. I much regret that General Meade's official report was not published in season to enable me to take full advantage, in preparing the brief sketch of the battles of the three days contained in this address. It reached me but the morning before it was sent to the press."

which greatly outnumbered his own, and had scarcely made his dispositions for the action when he fell, mortally wounded, at the head of his advance. The command of the First Corps devolved on General Doubleday, and that of the field on General Howard, who arrived at 11:30, with Schurz's and Barlow's divisions of the Eleventh Corps, the latter of whom received a severe wound. Thus strengthened, the advantage of the battle was for some time on our side. The attacks of the Rebels were vigorously repulsed by Wadsworth's division of the First Corps, and a large number of prisoners, including General Archer, were captured. At length, however, the continued reinforcement of the Confederates from the main body in the neighborhood, and by the divisions of Rodes and Early, coming down by separate lines from Heidlersberg and taking post on our extreme right, turned the fortunes of the day. Our army, after contesting the ground for five hours, was obliged to yield to the enemy, whose force outnumbered them two to one; and toward the close of the afternoon General Howard deemed it prudent to withdraw the two corps to the heights where we are now assembled. The great part of the First Corps passed through the outskirts of the town, and reached the hill without serious loss or molestation. The Eleventh Corps and portions of the First, not being aware that the enemy had already entered the town from the north, attempted to force their way through Washington and Baltimore streets, which, in the crowd and confusion of the scene, they did with a heavy loss in prisoners.

"General Howard was not unprepared for this turn in the fortunes of the day. He had, in the course of the morning, caused Cemetery Hill to be occupied by General Steinwehr, with the second division of the Eleventh Corps. About the time of the withdrawal of our troops to the hill, General Hancock arrived, having been sent by General

Meade, on hearing of the death of Reynolds, to assume the command of the field till he himself could reach the front. In conjunction with General Howard, General Hancock immediately proceeded to post the troops and to repel an attack on our right flank.   This attack was feebly made and promptly repulsed.   At nightfall, our troops on the hill, who had so gallantly sustained themselves during the toil and peril of the day, were cheered by the arrival of General Slocum with the Twelfth Corps and of General Sickles with a part of the Third.

"Such was the fortunes of the first day, commencing with decided success to our arms, followed by a check, but ending in the occupation of this all-important position.   To you, fellow citizens of Gettysburg, I need not attempt to portray the anxieties of the ensuing night.   Witnessing, as you had done with sorrow, the withdrawal of our army through your streets, with a considerable loss of prisoners— mourning as you did over the brave men who had fallen—shocked with the wide-spread desolation around you, of which the wanton burning of the Harman House had given the signal—ignorant of the near approach of General Meade, you passed the weary hours of the night in painful expectation.

"Long before the dawn of the 2d of July, the new Commander-in-Chief had reached the ever-memorable field of service and glory.   Having received intelligence of the events in progress, and informed by the reports of Generals Hancock and Howard of the favorable character of the positions, he determined to give battle to the enemy at this point.   He accordingly directed the remaining corps of the army to concentrate at Gettysburg with all possible expedition, and breaking up his head-quarters at Taneytown at ten P.M., he arrived at the front at one o'clock in the morning of the 2d of July.   Few were the moments given to sleep, during the rapid watches of that brief midsummer's night, by officers or men, though half of our troops were exhausted by the conflict of the day, and the residue wearied by the forced marches which had brought them to the rescue. The full moon, veiled by thin clouds, shone down that night on a strangely unwonted scene. The silence of the grave-yard was broken by the heavy tramp of armed men, by the neigh of the war-horse, the harsh rattle of the wheels of artillery hurrying to their stations, and all the indescribable tumult of preparation. The various corps of the army, as they arrived, were moved to their positions, on the spot where we are assembled and the ridges that extend south-east and south-west; batteries were planted and breastworks thrown up. The Second and Fifth Corps, with the rest of the Third, had reached the ground by seven o'clock, A.M.; but it was not till two o'clock in the afternoon that Sedgwick arrived with the Sixth Corps. He had marched thirty-four miles since nine o'clock on the evening before. It was only on his arrival that the Union army approached an equality of numbers with that of the Rebels, who were posted upon the opposite and parallel ridge, distant from a mile to a mile and a half, overlapping our position on either wing, and probably exceeding by ten thousand the army of General Meade.*

"And here I cannot but remark on the providential inaction of the Rebel army. Had the contest been renewed by it at daylight on the 2d of July, with the First and Eleventh Corps exhausted by the battle and the retreat, the Third and Twelfth weary from their forced march, and the

---

*"In the Address as originally prepared, judging from the best sources of information then within my reach, I assumed the equality of the two armies on the 2d and 3d of July. Subsequent inquiry has led me to think that I underrated somewhat the strength of Lee's force at Gettysburg, and I have corrected the text accordingly. General Halleck, however, in his official report accompanying the President's messages, states the armies to have been equal."

Second, Fifth and Sixth not yet arrived, nothing but a miracle could have saved the army from a great disaster. Instead of this, the day dawned, the sun rose, the cool hours of the morning passed, the forenoon and a considerable part of the afternoon wore away, without the slightest aggressive movement on the part of the enemy. Thus time was given for half of our forces to arrive and take their place in the lines, while the rest of the army enjoyed a much needed half day's repose.

"At length, between three and four o'clock in the afternoon, the work of death began. A signal gun from the hostile batteries was followed by a tremendous cannonade along the Rebel lines, and this by a heavy advance of infantry, brigade after brigade, commencing on the enemy's right against the left of our army, and so onward to the left center. A forward movement of General Sickles, to gain a commanding position from which to repel the Rebel attack, drew upon him a destructive fire from the enemy's batteries, and a furious assault from Longstreet's and Hill's advancing troops. After a brave resistance on the part of his corps, he was forced back, himself falling severely wounded. This was the critical moment of the second day; but the Fifth and part of the Sixth Corps, with portions of the First and Second, were promptly brought to the support of the Third. The struggle was fierce and murderous, but by sunset our success was decisive, and the enemy was driven back in confusion. The most important service was rendered towards the close of the day, in the memorable advance between Round Top and Little Round Top, by General Crawford's division of the Fifth Corps, consisting of two brigades of the Pennsylvania Reserves, of which one company was from this town and neighborhood. The Rebel force was driven back with great loss in killed and prisoners. At eight o'clock in the evening a desperate attempt was made by the enemy to storm the position of the Eleventh Corps on Cemetery Hill; but here, too, after a terrible conflict, he was repulsed with immense loss. Ewell, on our extreme right, which had been weakened by the withdrawal of the troops sent over to support our left, had succeeded in gaining a foothold within a portion of our lines, near Spangler's spring. This was the only advantage obtained by the Rebels to compensate them for the disasters of the day, and of this, as we shall see, they were soon deprived.

"Such was the result of the second act of this eventful drama,—a day hard fought, and at one moment anxious, but, with the exception of the slight reverse just named, crowned with dearly earned but uniform success to our arms, auspicious of a glorious termination of the final struggle. On these good omens the night fell.

"In the course of the night, General Geary returned to his position on the right, from which he had hastened the day before to strengthen the Third Corps. He immediately engaged the enemy, and, after a sharp and decisive action, drove them out of our lines, recovering the ground which had been lost on the preceding day. A spirited contest was kept up all the morning on this part of the line; but General Geary, reinforced by Wheaton's brigade of the Sixth Corps, maintained his position, and inflicted very severe losses on the Rebels.

"Such was the cheering commencement of the third day's work, and with it ended all serious attempts of the enemy on our right. As on the preceding day, his efforts were now mainly directed against our left centre and left wing. From eleven till half-past one o'clock, all was still— a solemn pause of preparation, as if both armies were nerving themselves for the supreme effort. At length the awful silence, more terrible than the wildest tumult of battle, was broken by the roar of two hundred and fifty pieces of artillery from the opposite ridges, joining in a cannonade of unsurpassed violence—the Rebel batteries along two-thirds of their line pouring their fire upon Cemetery Hill, and the centre and left wing of our army. Having attempted in this way for two hours, but without success, to shake the steadiness of our lines, the enemy rallied his forces for a last grand assault. Their attack was principally directed against the position of our Second Corps. Successive lines of Rebel infantry moved forward with equal spirit and steadiness from their cover on the wooded crest of Seminary Ridge, crossing the intervening plain, and, supported right and left by their choicest brigades, charged furiously up to our batteries. Our own brave troops of the Second Corps, supported by Doubleday's division and Stannard's brigade of the First, received the shock with firmness; the ground on both sides was long and fiercely contested, and was covered with the killed and the wounded; the tide of battle flowed and ebbed across the plain, till, after "a determined and gallant struggle," as it is pronounced by General Lee, the Rebel advance, consisting of two-thirds of Hill's corps and the whole of Longstreet's—including Pickett's division, the élite of his corps, which had not yet been under fire, and was now depended upon to decide the fortune of this last eventful day—was driven back with prodigious slaughter, discomfited and broken. While these events were in progress at our left centre, the enemy was driven, with a considerable loss of prisoners, from a strong position on our extreme left, from which he was annoying our force on Little Round Top. In the terrific assault on our centre, Generals Hancock and Gibbon were wounded. In the Rebel army, Generals Armistead, Kemper, Pettigrew and Trimble were wounded, the first named mortally, the latter also made prisoner, General

Garnett was killed, and thirty-five hundred officers and men made prisoners.

"These were the expiring agonies of the three days' conflict, and with them the battle ceased. It was fought by the Union army with courage and skill, from the first cavalry skirmish on Wednesday morning to the fearful route of the enemy on Friday afternoon, by every arm and every rank of the service, by officers and men, by cavalry, artillery, and infantry. The superiority of numbers was with the enemy, who were led by the ablest commanders in their service; and if the Union force had the advantage of a strong position, the Confederates had that of choosing time and place, the prestige of former victories over the army of the Potomac, and of the success of the first day. Victory does not always fall to the lot of those who deserve it; but that so decisive a triumph, under circumstances like these, was gained by our troops, I would ascribe, under Providence, to the spirit of exalted patriotism that animated them, and the consciousness that they were fighting in a righteous cause.

"All hope of defeating our army, and securing what General Lee calls 'the valuable results' of such an achievement, having vanished, he thought only of rescuing from destruction the remains of his shattered forces. In killed, wounded and missing, he had, as far as can be ascertained, suffered a loss of about 37,000 men—rather more than a third of the army with which he is supposed to have marched into Pennsylvania. Perceiving that his only safety was in rapid retreat, he commenced withdrawing his troops at daybreak on the 4th, throwing up field works in front of our left, which, assuming the appearance of a new position, were intended probably to protect the rear of his army in retreat. That day—sad celebration of the 4th of July for an army of Americans—was passed by him in hurrying

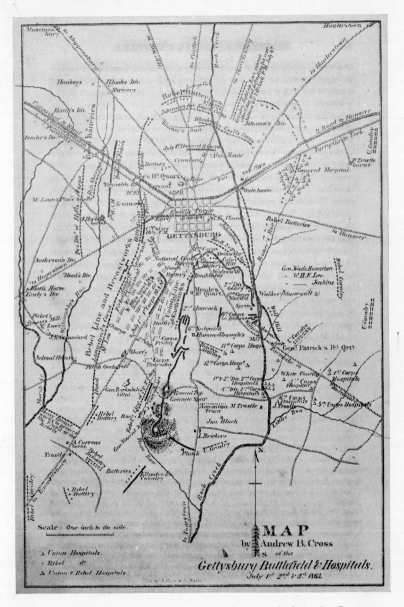

Map of Gettysburg battle-field and hospitals by Andrew B. Cross as
published in the official report, 1863

off his trains. By nightfall, the main army was in full retreat upon the Cashtown and Fairfield roads, and it moved with such precipitation, that, short as the nights were, by day-light the following morning, notwithstanding a heavy rain, the rear guard had left its position. The struggle of the last two days resembled, in many respects, the battle of Waterloo; and if, in the evening of the third day, General Meade, like the Duke of Wellington, had had the assistance of a powerful auxiliary army to take up the pursuit, the route of the Rebels would have been as complete as that of Napoleon.

"Owing to the circumstances just named, the intentions of the enemy were not apparent on the 4th. The moment his retreat was discovered, the following morning, he was pursued by our cavalry on the Cashtown road and through the Emmitsburg and Monterey passes, and by Sedgwick's corps on the Fairfield road. His rear guard was briskly attacked at Fairfield; a great number of wagons and ambulances were captured in the passes of the mountains; the country swarmed with his stragglers, and his wounded were literally emptied from the vehicles containing them into the farm houses on the road. General Lee, in his report, makes repeated mention of the Union prisoners whom he conveyed into Virginia, somewhat overstating their number. He states, also, that 'such of his wounded as were in a condition to be removed' were forwarded to Williamsport. He does not mention that the number of his wounded *not* removed, and left to the Christian care of the victors, was 7,540, not one of whom failed of any attention which it was possible, under the circumstances of the case, to afford them, not one of whom, certainly, has been put upon Libby prison fare—lingering death by starvation. Heaven forbid, however, that we should claim any merit for the exercise of common humanity.

"Under the protection of the mountain ridge, whose
narrow passes are easily held even by a retreating army,
General Lee reached Williamsport in safety, and took up a
strong position opposite to that place.   General Meade
necessarily pursued with the main army by a flank movement through Middletown, Turner's Pass having been secured by General French.   Passing through the South
mountain, the Union army came up with that of the Rebels
on the 12th, and found it securely posted on the heights of
Marsh run.   The position was reconnoitred, and preparations made for an attack on the 13th.   The depth of the
river, swollen by the recent rains, authorized the expectation that the enemy would be brought to a general engage-
ment the following day.   An advance was accordingly made
by General Meade on the morning of the 14th; but it was
soon found that the Rebels had escaped in the night, with
such haste that Ewell's corps forded the river where the
water was breast-high.   The cavalry, which had rendered
the most important services during the three days, and in
harassing the enemy's retreat, was now sent in pursuit, and
captured two guns and a large number of prisoners.   In an
action which took place at Falling Waters, General Pettigrew was mortally wounded.   General Meade, in further
pursuit of the Rebels, crossed the Potomac at Berlin.   Thus
again covering the approaches to Washington, he compelled
the enemy to pass the Blue Ridge at one of the upper gaps;
and in about six weeks from the commencement of the campaign, General Lee found himself on the south side of the
Rappahannock, with the probable loss of about a third part
of his army.

"Such, most inadequately recounted, is the history of
the ever-memorable three days, and of the events immediately preceding and following.   It has been pretended, in
order to diminish the magnitude of this disaster to the

Rebel cause, that it was merely the repulse of an attack on a strongly defended position. The tremendous losses on both sides are a sufficient answer to this misrepresentation, and attest the courage and obstinacy with which the three days' battle was waged. Few of the great conflicts of modern times have cost victors and vanquished so great a sacrifice. On the Union side there fell, in the whole campaign, of generals killed, Reynolds, Weed and Zook, and wounded, Barlow, Barnes, Butterfield, Doubleday, Gibbon, Graham, Hancock, Sickles and Warren; while of officers below the rank of General, and men, there were 2,834 killed, 13,709 wounded, and 6,643 missing. On the Confederate side, there were killed on the field or mortally wounded, Generals Armistead, Barksdale, Garnett, Pender, Pettigrew and Semmes, and wounded, Heth, Hood, Johnson, Kemper, Kimball and Trimble. Of officers below the rank of general, and men, there were taken prisoners, including the wounded, 13,621, an amount ascertained officially. Of the wounded in a condition to be removed, of the killed and the missing, the enemy has made no report. They are estimated, from the best data which the nature of the case admits, at 23,000. General Meade also captured 3 cannon, and 41 standards; and 24,978 small arms were collected on the battle-field.

"I must leave to others, who can do it from personal observation, to describe the mournful spectacle presented by these hill-sides and plains at the close of the terrible conflict. It was a saying of the Duke of Wellington, that next to a defeat, the saddest thing was a victory. The horrors of the battle field, after the contest is over, the sights and sounds of woe,—let me throw a pall over the scene, which no words can adequately depict to those who have not witnessed it, on which no one who has witnessed it, and who has a heart in his bosom, can bear to dwell. One drop of balm alone, one drop of heavenly, life-giving balm, mingles in this bitter cup of misery. Scarcely has the cannon ceased to roar, when the brethren and sisters of Christian benevolence, ministers of compassion, angels of pity, hasten to the field and the hospital, to moisten the parched tongue, to bind the ghastly wounds, to soothe the parting agonies alike of friend and foe, and to catch the last whispered messages of love from dying lips. 'Carry this miniature back to my dear wife, but do not take it from my bosom till I am gone.' 'Tell my little sister not to grieve for me; I am willing to die for my country.' 'Oh, that my mother were here!' When, since Aaron stood between the living and the dead, was there ever so gracious a ministry as this? It has been said that it is characteristic of Americans to treat women with a deference not paid to them in any other country. I will not undertake to say whether this is so; but I will say, that, since this terrible war has been waged, the women of the loyal States, if never before, have entitled themselves to our highest admiration and gratitude,—alike those who at home, often with fingers unused to the toil, often bowed beneath their own domestic cares, have performed an amount of daily labor not exceeded by those who work for their daily bread, and those who, in the hospital and the tents of the Sanitary and Christian Commissions, have rendered services which millions could not buy. Happily, the labor and the service are their own reward. Thousands of matrons and thousands of maidens have experienced a delight in these homely toils and services, compared with which the pleasures of the ball room and the opera house are tame and unsatisfactory. This, on earth, is reward enough, but a richer is in store for them. Yes, brothers, sisters of charity, while you bind up the wounds of the poor sufferers—the humblest, perhaps, that have shed their blood for the country—forget not Who it is that will hereafter say to you, 'Inasmuch as ye have done it unto one of the least of these my brethren, ye have done it unto me.'

"And now, friends, fellow citizens, as we stand among these honored graves, the momentous question presents itself: Which of the two parties to the war is responsible for all this suffering, for this dreadful sacrifice of life, the lawful and constitutional government of the United States, or the ambitious men who have rebelled against it? I say 'rebelled' against it, although Earl Russell, the British Secretary of State for Foreign Affairs, in his recent temperate and conciliatory speech in Scotland, seems to intimate that no prejudice ought to attach to that word, inasmuch as our English forefathers rebelled against Charles I. and James II., and our American fathers rebelled against George III. These, certainly, are venerable precedents, but they prove only that it is just and proper to rebel against oppressive governments. They do not prove that it was just and proper for the son of James II. to rebel against George I., or his grandson Charles Edward to rebel against George II.; nor, as it seems to me, ought these dynastic struggles, little better than family quarrels, to be compared with this monstrous conspiracy against the American Union. These precedents do not prove that it was just and proper for the 'disappointed great men' of the cotton-growing States to rebel against 'the most beneficent government of which history gives us any account,' as the Vice President of the Confederacy, in November, 1860, charged them with doing. They do not create a presumption even in favor of the disloyal slaveholders of the South, who, living under a government of which Mr. Jefferson Davis, in the session of 1860-61, said that it 'was the best government ever instituted by man, unexceptionably administered, and under which the people have been prosperous beyond comparison with any other people whose career has been recorded in history,' rebelled against it because their aspiring politicians, himself among the rest, were in danger of losing their monopoly of its offices.—What would have been thought by an impartial posterity of the American rebellion against George III., if the colonists had at all times been more than equally represented in parliament, and James Otis, and Patrick Henry, and Washington, and Franklin, and the Adamses, and Hancock, and Jefferson, and men of their stamp, had for two generations enjoyed the confidence of the sovereign and administered the government of the empire? What would have been thought of the rebellion against Charles I., if Cromwell, and the men of his school, had been the responsible advisers of that prince from his accession to the throne, and then, on account of a partial change in the ministry, had brought his head to the block, and involved the country in a desolating war, for the sake of dismembering it and establishing a new government south of the Trent? What would have been thought of the Whigs of 1688, if they had themselves composed the cabinet of James II., and been the advisers of the measures and the promoters of the policy which drove him into exile? The Puritans of 1640, and the Whigs of 1688, rebelled against arbitrary power in order to establish constitutional liberty. If they had risen against Charles and James because those monarchs favored equal rights, and in order themselves, 'for the first time in the history of the world,' to establish an oligarchy 'founded on the corner-stone of slavery,' they would truly have furnished a precedent for the Rebels of the South, but their cause would not have been sustained by the eloquence of Pym, or of Somers, nor sealed with the blood of Hampden or Russell.

"I call the war which the Confederates are waging against the Union a 'rebellion,' because it is one, and in grave matters it is best to call things by their right names.

I speak of it as a crime, because the Constitution of the United States so regards it, and puts 'rebellion' on a par with 'invasion.' The Constitution and law not only of England, but of every civilized country, regard them in the same light; or rather they consider the rebel in arms as far worse than the alien enemy. To levy war against the United States is the constitutional definition of treason, and that crime is by every civilized government regarded as the highest which citizen or subject can commit. Not content with the sanctions of human justice, of all the crimes against the law of the land it is singled out for the denunciations of religion. The litanies of every church in Christendom whose ritual embraces that office, as far as I am aware, from the metropolitan cathedrals of Europe to the humblest missionary chapel in the islands of the sea, concur with the Church of England in imploring the Sovereign of the Universe, by the most awful adjurations which the heart of man can conceive or his tongue utter, to deliver us from 'sedition, privy conspiracy and rebellion.' And reason good; for while a rebellion against tyranny—a rebellion designed, after prostrating arbitrary power, to establish free government on the basis of justice and truth—is an enterprise on which good men and angels may look with complacency, an unprovoked rebellion of ambitious men against a beneficent government, for the purpose—the avowed purpose—of establishing, extending and perpetuating any form of injustice and wrong, is an imitation on earth of that first foul revolt of "the Infernal Serpent," against which the Supreme Majesty sent forth the armed myriads of his angels, and clothed the right arm of his Son with the three-bolted thunders of omnipotence.

"Lord Bacon, in 'the true marshalling of the sovereign degrees of honor,' assigns the first place to 'the *Conditores Imperiorum,* founders of States and Commonwealths;' and,

truly, to build up from the discordant elements of our nature, the passions, the interests and the opinions of the
individual man, the rivalries of family, clan and tribe, the
influences of climate and geographical position, the acci-
dents of peace and war accumulated for ages—to build up
from these oftentimes warring elements a well-compacted,
prosperous and powerful State, if it were to be accomplished
by one effort or in one generation, would require a more
than mortal skill. To contribute in some notable degree to
this, the greatest work of man, by wise and patriotic council
in peace and loyal heroism in war, is as high as human
merit can well rise, and far more than to any of those to
whom Bacon assigns this highest place of honor, whose
names can hardly be repeated without a wondering smile—
Romulus, Cyrus, Cæsar, Ottoman, Ismael—is it due to our
Washington, as the founder of the American Union. But
if to achieve or help to achieve this greatest work of man's
wisdom and virtue gives title to a place among the chief ben-
efactors, rightful heirs of the benedictions, of mankind, by
equal reason shall the bold, bad men who seek to undo the
noble work, *Eversores Imperiorum,* destroyers of States,
who for base and selfish ends rebel against beneficent governments, seek to overturn wise constitutions, to lay powerful republican Unions at the foot of foreign thrones, to
bring on civil and foreign war, anarchy at home, dictation
abroad, desolation, ruin—by equal reason, I say, yes, a
thousandfold stronger shall they inherit the execrations of
the ages.

"But to hide the deformity of the crime under the cloak
of that sophistry which strives to make the worse appear
the better reason, we are told by the leaders of the Rebellion that in our complex system of government the separate
States are 'sovereigns,' and that the central power is only
an 'agency' established by these sovereigns to manage cer-

tain little affairs—such, forsooth, as Peace, War, Army, Navy, Finance, Territory, and Relations with the native tribes—which they could not so conveniently administer themselves. It happens, unfortunately for this theory, that the Federal Constitution (which has been adopted by the people of every State of the Union as much as their own State constitutions have been adopted, and is declared to be paramount to them) nowhere recognizes the States as 'sovereigns'—in fact, that, by their names, it does not recognize them at all; while the authority established by that instrument is recognized, in its text, not as an 'agency,' but as 'the Government of the United States.' By that Constitution, moreover, which purports in its preamble to be ordained and established by 'the People of the United States,' it is expressly provided, that 'the members of the State legislatures, and all executive and judicial officers, shall be bound by oath or affirmation to support the Constitution.' Now it is a common thing, under all governments, for an agent to be bound by oath to be faithful to his sovereign; but I never heard before of sovereigns being bound by oath to be faithful to their agency.

"Certainly I do not deny that the separate States are clothed with sovereign powers for the administration of local affairs. It is one of the most beautiful features of our mixed system of government; but it is equally true, that, in adopting the Federal Constitution, the States abdicated, by express renunciation, all the most important functions of national sovereignty, and, by one comprehensive, self-denying clause, gave up all right to contravene the Constitution of the United States. Specifically, and by enumeration, they renounced all the most important prerogatives of independent States for peace and for war,—the right to keep troops or ships of war in time of peace, or to engage in war unless actually invaded; to enter into compact with another

State or a foreign power; to lay any duty on tonnage, or any impost on exports or imports, without the consent of Congress; to enter into any treaty, alliance, or confederation; to grant letters of marque and reprisal, and to emit bills of credit—while all these powers and many others are expressly vested in the General Government. To ascribe to political communities, thus limited in their jurisdiction—who cannot even establish a post office on their own soil—the character of independent sovereignty, and to reduce a national organization, clothed with all the transcendent powers of government, to the name and condition of an 'agency' of the States, proves nothing but that the logic of secession is on a par with its loyalty and patriotism.

"Oh, but 'the reserved rights!' And what of the reserved rights? The tenth amendment of the Constitution, supposed to provide for 'reserved rights,' is constantly misquoted. By that amendment, 'the *powers* not delegated to the United States by the Constitution, nor prohibited by it to the States, are reserved to the States respectively, or to the people.' The 'powers' reserved must of course be such as could have been, but were not delegated to the United States,—could have been, but were not prohibited to the States; but to speak of the *right* of an *individual* State to secede, as a *power* that could have been, though it was not delegated to the *United States,* is simple nonsense.

"But waiving this obvious absurdity, can it need a serious argument to prove that there can be no State right to enter into a new confederation reserved under a constitution which expressly prohibits a State to 'enter into any treaty, alliance, or confederation,' or any 'agreement or compact with another State or a foreign power?' To say that the State may, by enacting the preliminary farce of secession, acquire the right to do the prohibited things—to say, for instance, that though the States, in forming the

Constitution, delegated to the United States and prohibited
to themselves the power of declaring war, there was by
implication reserved to each State the right of seceding and
then declaring war; that, though they expressly prohibited
to the States and delegated to the United States the entire
treaty-making power, they reserved by implication (for an
express reservation is not pretended) to the individual
States, to Florida, for instance, the right to secede, and then
to make a treaty with Spain retroceding that Spanish col-
ony, and thus surrendering to a foreign power the key to
the Gulf of Mexico,—to maintain propositions like these,
with whatever affected seriousness it is done, appears to me
egregious trifling.

"Pardon me, my friends, for dwelling on these wretched
sophistries. But it is these which conducted the armed hosts
of rebellion to your doors on the terrible and glorious days
of July, and which have brought upon the whole land the
scourge of an aggressive and wicked war—a war which can
have no other termination compatible with the permanent
safety and welfare of the country but the complete destruction of the military power of the enemy. I have, on other
occasions, attempted to show that to yield to his demands
and acknowledge his independence, thus resolving the
Union at once into two hostile governments, with a cer-
tainty of further disintegration, would annihilate the
strength and the influence of the country as a member of the
family of nations; afford to foreign powers the opportunity
and the temptation for humiliating and disastrous interfer-
ence in our affairs; wrest from the Middle and Western
States some of their great natural outlets to the sea and of
their most important lines of internal communication; de-
prive the commerce and navigation of the country of two-
thirds of our sea coast and of the fortresses which protect
it; not only so, but would enable each individual State—

some of them with a white population equal to a good sized
Northern county—or rather the dominant party in each
State, to cede its territory, its harbors, its fortresses, the
mouths of its rivers, to any foreign power. It cannot be
that the people of the loyal States—that twenty-two millions of brave and prosperous freemen—will, for the temptation of a brief truce in an eternal border war, consent to
this hideous national suicide.

"Do not think that I exaggerate the consequences of
yielding to the demands of the leaders of the rebellion. I
understate them. They require of us not only all the sacrifices I have named, not only the cession to them, a foreign
and hostile power, of all the territory of the United States
at present occupied by the Rebel forces, but the abandon-
ment to them of the vast regions we have rescued from their
grasp—of Maryland, of a part of Eastern Virginia and the
whole of Western Virginia; the sea coast of North and
South Carolina, Georgia, and Florida; Kentucky, Tennessee, and Missouri; Arkansas, and the larger portion of
Mississippi, Louisiana, and Texas—in most of which, with
the exception of lawless guerillas, there is not a Rebel in
arms, in all of which the great majority of the people are
loyal to the Union. We must give back, too, the helpless
colored population, thousands of whom are perilling their
lives in the ranks of our armies, to a bondage rendered ten-
fold more bitter by the momentary enjoyment of freedom.
Finally, we must surrender every man in the Southern country, white or black, who has moved a finger or spoken a
word for the restoration of the Union, to a reign of terror
as remorseless as that of Robespierre, which has been the
chief instrument by which the Rebellion has been organized
and sustained, and which has already filled the prisons of
the South with noble men, whose only crime is that they are
not the worst of criminals. The South is full of such men.

I do not believe there has been a day since the election of
President Lincoln, when, if an ordinance of secession could
have been fairly submitted, after a free discussion, to the
mass of the people in any single Southern State, a majority
of ballots would have been given in its favor. No, not in
South Carolina. It is not possible that the majority of the
people, even of that State, if permitted, without fear or
favor, to give a ballot on the question, would have abandoned a leader like Petigru, and all the memories of the
Gadsdens, the Rutledges, and the Cotesworth Pinckneys of
the revolutionary and constitutional age, to follow the agi-
tators of the present day.

"Nor must we be deterred from the vigorous prosecution of the war by the suggestion, continually thrown out
by the Rebels and those who sympathize with them, that,
however it might have been at an earlier stage, there has
been engendered by the operations of the war a state of
exasperation and bitterness which, independent of all reference to the original nature of the matters in controversy,
will forever prevent the restoration of the Union, and the
return of harmony between the two great sections of the
country. This opinion I take to be entirely without
foundation.

"No man can deplore more than I do the miseries of
every kind unavoidably incident to war. Who could stand
on this spot and call to mind the scenes of the first days of
July with any other feeling? A sad foreboding of what
would ensue, if war should break out between North and
South, has haunted me through life, and led me, perhaps
too long, to tread in the path of hopeless compromise, in
the fond endeavor to conciliate those who were predeter-
mined not to be conciliated. But it is not true, as is pretended by the Rebels and their sympathizers, that the war
has been carried on by the United States without entire re-

gard to those temperaments which are enjoined by the law
of nations, by our modern civilization, and by the spirit of
Christianity. It would be quite easy to point out, in the
recent military history of the leading European powers, acts
of violence and cruelty, in the prosecution of their wars, to
which no parallel can be found among us. In fact, when
we consider the peculiar bitterness with which civil wars are
almost invariably waged, we may justly boast of the manner in which the United States have carried on the contest.
It is of course impossible to prevent the lawless acts of
stragglers and deserters, or the occasional unwarrantable
proceedings of subordinates on distant stations; but I do not
believe there is, in all history, the record of a civil war of
such gigantic dimensions where so little has been done in the
spirit of vindictiveness as in this war, by the Government
and commanders of the United States; and this notwithstanding the provocation given by the Rebel Government
by assuming the responsibility of wretches like Quantrell,
refusing quarter to colored troops and scourging and selling
into slavery free colored men from the North who fall into
their hands, by covering the sea with pirates, refusing a just
exchange of prisoners, while they crowd their armies with
paroled prisoners not exchanged, and starving prisoners of
war to death.

"In the next place, if there are any present who believe
that, in addition to the effect of the military operations of
the war, the confiscation acts and emancipation proclamations have embittered the Rebels beyond the possibility of
reconciliation, I would request them to reflect that the tone
of the Rebel leaders and Rebel press was just as bitter in
the first months of the war, nay, before a gun was fired, as
it is now. There were speeches made in Congress in the
very last session before the outbreak of the Rebellion, so
ferocious as to show that their authors were under the in-

fluence of a real frenzy. At the present day, if there is any discrimination made by the Confederate press in the affected scorn, hatred and contumely with which every shade of opinion and sentiment in the loyal States is treated, the bitterest contempt is bestowed upon those at the North who still speak the language of compromise, and who condemn those measures of the administration which are alleged to have rendered the return of peace hopeless.

"No, my friends, that gracious Providence which overrules all things for the best, 'from seeming evil still educing good,' has so constituted our natures, that the violent excitement of the passions in one direction is generally followed by a reaction in an opposite direction, and the sooner for the violence. If it were not so—if injuries inflicted and retaliated of necessity led to new retaliations, with forever accumulating compound interest of revenge, then the world, thousands of years ago, would have been turned into an earthly hell, and the nations of the earth would have been resolved into clans of furies and demons, each forever warring with his neighbor. But it is not so; all history teaches a different lesson. The Wars of the Roses in England lasted an entire generation, from the battle of St. Albans in 1455 to that of Bosworth Field in 1485. Speaking of the former, Hume says: 'This was the first blood spilt in that fatal quarrel, which was not finished in less than a course of thirty years; which was signalized by twelve pitched battles: which opened a scene of extraordinary fierceness and cruelty; is computed to have cost the lives of eighty princes of the blood; and almost entirely annihilated the ancient nobility of England. The strong attachments which, at that time, men of the same kindred bore to each other, and the vindictive spirit which was considered a point of honor, rendered the great families implacable in their resentment, and widened every moment the breach between the parties.' Such was the state of things in England under which an entire generation grew up; but when Henry VII., in whom the titles of the two Houses were united, went up to London after the battle of Bosworth Field, to mount the throne, he was everywhere received with joyous acclamations, 'as one ordained and sent from heaven to put an end to the dissensions' which had so long afflicted the country.

"The great rebellion of England of the seventeenth century, after long and angry premonitions, may be said to have begun with the calling of the Long Parliament in 1640, and to have ended with the return of Charles II., in 1660—twenty years of discord, conflict and civil war; of confiscation, plunder, havoc; a proud hereditary peerage trampled in the dust; a national church overturned, its clergy beggared, its most eminent prelate put to death; a military despotism established on the ruins of a monarchy which had subsisted seven hundred years, and the legitimate sovereign brought to the block; the great families which adhered to the king proscribed, impoverished, ruined; prisoners of war—a fate worse than starvation in Libby—sold to slavery in the West Indies; in a word, everything that can embitter and madden contending factions. Such was the state of things for twenty years; and yet, by no gentle transition, but suddenly, and 'when the restoration of affairs appeared most hopeless,' the son of the beheaded sovereign was brought back to his father's blood-stained throne, with such 'unexpressible and universal joy' as led the merry monarch to exclaim, 'he doubted it had been his own fault he had been absent so long, for he saw nobody who did not protest he had ever wished for his return.' 'In this wonderful manner,' says Clarendon, 'and with this incredible expedition did God put an end to a rebellion that had raged near twenty years, and had been carried on with all the horrid circumstances of murder, devastation and parracide that fire and sword, in the hands of the most wicked men in the world,' (it is a royalist that is speaking,) 'could be instruments of, almost to the desolation of two kingdoms, and the exceeding defacing and deforming of the third. . . . By these remarkable steps did the merciful hand of God, in this short space of time, not only bind up and heal all those wounds, but even made the scar as undiscernable as, in respect of the deepness, was possible, which was a glorious addition to the deliverance.'

"In Germany, the wars of the Reformation and of Charles V., in the sixteenth century, the Thirty Years' war in the seventeenth century, the Seven Years' war in the eighteenth century, not to speak of other less celebrated contests, entailed upon that country all the miseries of intestine strife for more than three centuries. At the close of the last named war—which was the shortest of all, and waged in the most civilized age—'an officer,' says Archenholz, 'rode through seven villages in Hesse, and found in them but one human being.' More than three hundred principalities, comprehended in the Empire, fermented with the fierce passions of proud and petty States; at the commencement of this period the castles of robber counts frowned upon every hill-top; a dreadful secret tribunal, whose seat no one knew, whose power none could escape, froze the hearts of men with terror throughout the land; religious hatred mingled its bitter poison in the seething caldron of provincial animosity; but of all these deadly enmities between the States of Germany scarcely the memory remains. There are controversies in that country, at the present day, but they grow mainly out of the rivalry of the two leading powers. There is no country in the world in which the sentiment of national brotherhood is stronger.

"In Italy, on the breaking up of the Roman Empire, society might be said to be resolved into its original elements—into hostile atoms, whose only movement was that of mutual repulsion. Ruthless barbarians had destroyed the old organizations, and covered the land with a merciless feudalism. As the new civilization grew up, under the wing of the church, the noble families and the walled towns fell madly into conflict with each other; the secular feud of Pope and Emperor scourged the land; province against province, city against city, street against street, waged remorseless war with each other from father to son, till Dante was able to fill his imaginary hell with the real demons of Italian history. So ferocious had the factions become, that the great poet-exile himself, the glory of his native city and of his native language, was, by a decree of the municipality, condemned to be burned alive if found in the city of Florence. But these deadly feuds and hatred yielded to political influences, as the hostile cities were grouped into States under stable governments; the lingering traditions of the ancient animosities gradually died away, and now Tuscan and Lombard, Sardinian and Neapolitan, as if to shame the degenerate sons of America, are joining in one cry for a united Italy.

"In France, not to go back to the civil wars of the League, in the sixteenth century, and of the Fronde, in the seventeenth; not to speak of the dreadful scenes throughout the kingdom, which followed the revocation of the edict of Nantes; we have, in the great revolution which commenced at the close of the last century, seen the blood-hounds of civil strife let loose as rarely before in the history of the world. The reign of terror established at Paris stretched its bloody Briarean arms to every city and village in the land, and if the most deadly feuds which ever divided a people had the power to cause permanent alienation and hatred, this surely was the occasion. But far otherwise the fact. In seven years from the fall of Robespierre, the strong arm of the youthful conquerer brought order out of this chaos of crime and woe; Jacobins whose hands were scarcely cleansed from the best blood of France met the returning emigrants, whose estates they had confiscated and whose kindred they had dragged to the guillotine, in the Imperial antechambers; and when, after another turn of the wheel of fortune, Louis XVIII. was restored to his throne, he took the regicide Fouche, who had voted for his brother's death, to his cabinet and confidence.

"The people of loyal America will never ask you, sir, to take to your confidence or admit again to a share in the government the hard-hearted men whose cruel lust of power has brought this desolating war upon the land, but there is no personal bitterness felt even against them. They may live, if they can bear to live after wantonly causing the death of so many thousands of their fellow-men; they may live in safe obscurity beneath the shelter of the government they have sought to overthrow, or they may fly to the protection of the governments of Europe—some of them are already there, seeking, happily in vain, to obtain the aid of foreign powers in furtherance of their own treason. There let them stay. The humblest dead soldier, that lies cold and stiff in his grave before us, is an object of envy beneath the clods that cover him, in comparison with the living man, I care not with what trumpery credentials he may be furnished, who is willing to grovel at the foot of a foreign throne for assistance in compassing the ruin of his country.

"But the hour is coming and now is, when the power of the leaders of the Rebellion to delude and inflame must cease. There is no bitterness on the part of the masses. The people of the South are not going to wage an eternal war, for the wretched pretext by which this Rebellion is sought to be justified. The bonds that unite us as one people—a substantial community of origin, language, belief, and law, (the four great ties that hold the societies of men together;) common national and political interests; a common history; a common pride in a glorious ancestry; a common interest in this great heritage of blessings; the very geographical features of the country; the mighty rivers that cross the lines of climate and thus facilitate the interchange of natural and industrial products, while the wonder-working arm of the engineer has levelled the mountain-walls which separate the East and West, compelling your own Alleghenies, my Maryland and Pennsylvania friends, to open wide their everlasting doors to the chariot-wheels of traffic and travel; these bonds of union are of perennial force and energy, while the causes of alienation are imaginary, factitious, and transient. The heart of the people, North and South, is for the Union. Indications, too plain to be mistaken, announce the fact, both in the East and the West of the States in rebellion. In North Carolina and Arkansas the fatal charm at length is broken. At Raleigh and Little Rock the lips of honest and brave men are unsealed, and an independent press is unlimbering its artillery. When its rifled cannon shall begin to roar, the hosts of treasonable sophistry—the mad delusions of the day—will fly like the Rebel army through the passes of yonder mountain. The weary masses of the people are yearning to see the dear old flag again floating upon their capitols, and they sigh for the return of the peace, prosperity, and happiness, which they enjoyed under a government whose power was felt only in its blessings.

"And now, friends, fellow citizens of Gettysburg and Pennsylvania, and you from remoter States, let me again, as we part, invoke your benediction on these honored graves. You feel, though the occasion is mournful, that it is good to be here. You feel that it was greatly auspicious for the cause of the country, that the men of the East and the men of the West, the men of nineteen sister States, stood side by side, on the perilous ridges of the battle. You now feel it a new bond of union, that they shall lie side by side, till the clarion, louder than that which marshalled them to the combat, shall awake their slumbers. God bless the Union; it is dearer to us for the blood of brave men which has been shed in its defence. The spots on which they stood and fell; these pleasant heights; the fertile plain beneath them; the thriving village whose streets so lately rang with the strange din of war; the fields beyond the ridge, where the noble Reynolds held the advancing foe at bay, and, while he gave up his own life, assured by his forethought and self-sacrifice the triumph of the two succeeding days; the little streams which wind through the hills, on whose banks in after-times the wondering ploughmen will turn up, with the rude weapons of savage warfare, the fearful missiles of modern artillery; Seminary Ridge, the Peach Orchard, Cemetery, Culp, and Wolf Hill, Round Top, Little Round Top, humble names, henceforward dear and famous—no lapse of time, no distance of space, shall cause you to be forgotten. 'The whole earth,' said Pericles, as he stood over the remains of his fellow citizens, who had fallen in the first year of the Peloponnesian war, 'the whole earth is the sepulchre of illustrious men.' All time, he might have added, is the millennium of their glory. Surely I would do no injustice to the other noble achievements of the war, which have reflected such honor on both arms of the service, and have entitled the armies and the navy of the United states, their officers and men, to the warmest thanks and the richest rewards which a grateful people can pay. But they, I am sure, will join us in saying, as we bid farewell to the dust of these martyr-heroes, that wheresoever throughout the civilized world the accounts of this great warfare are read, and down to the latest period of recorded time, in the glorious annals of our common country, there will be no brighter page than that which relates The Battles of Gettysburg."

THE END

INDEX

INDEX

257

Thi b